Mental Toughness

How to Build a Strong Mindset and Achieve Your Goals

(How to Develop a Resilient Mind, Character and Personality Away From Fear Stress and Anxiety)

Domingo Adcock

Published By **Regina Loviusher**

Domingo Adcock

*Mental Toughness: How to Build a Strong Mindset
and Achieve Your Goals (How to Develop a
Resilient Mind, Character and Personality Away
From Fear Stress and Anxiety)*

ISBN   978-1-998927-56-2

Legal & Disclaimer

Table Of Contents

Chapter 1: Mental Toughness

Before we bypass similarly on this healthy statistics about intellectual durability, let us visualize what we suggest by manner of being mentally difficult. Hence, what is mental sturdiness?

Mental Toughness is an evaluation of someone or an man or woman's capability to emerge as resilient and being self assure that permeates the very cradle of success and actually becoming a success in any lifestyles's endeavors which includes, education, sports activities, place of job, profession, enterprise, generation, information, technology, and lots of others.

As a huge standards the emergence of severa sports in the global introduced about highbrow durability specifically in sports activities, profession, schooling, industrial agency and many others. The thoughts additionally begins offevolved in the route of the period of training of an man or woman to grow to be a higher person among pairs or corporations or as a scholar who is undergoing a few form of training.

However, it's far really worth of notice that the definition of Mental sturdiness might also range from the brilliant elements of view from super specialists who're in the area of agency, sports activities, generation, politics, education and so forth. But all of them have one trouble in not unusual and that is an individual need to be involved in intellectual durability.

Application of Mental sturdiness in sports sports;

From the Sports psychologist point of view, they see mental durability from an athlete issue of view, that the athletes dreams mental durability to undergo the numerous rigorous schooling time desk, as a way to compete with special athletes and to make bigger his or her capability to have a place over his combatants.

The sports activities sports psychologist believes that the onus is on the athlete to keep a top diploma to have the urge and hunger to prevail at every thing in time, the athlete want to additionally believe that he or she is able to making it display up. The sports psychologist desires the athlete to usually have a winning mentality and accept as actual with that she or he has an problem over amazing athletes. The duty to win should constantly reverberate inside the mind of the athlete in particular within the direction of competitions.

In the modern-day years, we have seen many businesses inside the worldwide of sports the usage of the offerings of a sports activities psychologist, why? Because they do not forget modern-day athletes now want intellectual decorate in any opposition or in their career at the same time as they play for the group.

This is real as various human beings inside the international of sports activities who are elite athletes doing some distance higher than their contemporaries. Some of the attributes of the elite athlete which makes them higher than others are in reality due to the reality they determined themselves and that they hold to expand themselves to rediscover themselves, they spend extra time training on their trade and continuously preserve a high degree of place, they constantly make sure that they live faraway from scandals, they continually make efforts to govern their sports activities and maximize their largest potentials.

The winning mentality does now not exchange in them and that they generally need greater, they don't commonly provide room for complacency and that they take each recreation significantly and normally live targeted. These are the severa attributes that differentiates the normal athlete from the elite and of path the ones sports activities typically comes with incredible rewards.

Mental durability within the education zone

The academic zone is not disregarded in intellectual toughness. As you could see in numerous college curriculums, schools have coated out diverse topics in conjunction with everyday assignments to be able to make the scholars to take a look at and ensure they may be able to carry out assignments and additionally keep them busy. Any scholar who isn't always able to deal with those sports activities sports will in all likelihood no longer do properly with regards to schooling. But if they have to find out themselves via one-of-a-kind method, which includes sports sports, skills in high-quality areas of lifestyles, then they may truely degree up or supersede their contemporaries.

Being the fine university university students occasionally doesn't mean you'll make more money extra than others or turn out to be a achievement more than others, Bill Gates for instance isn't always a professor but of course he is through a long way richer than lots and heaps of professors inside the international. Mark Zuckernberg the owner of fb doesn't have any production enterprise but with fb he's the diverse top 5 billionaires that we've were given in the international these days.

Hence, is all approximately coming across your capability and growth your mental durability to accumulate your desires.

We have individuals within the international these days who've been capable of do exploits and are certainly in advance of their pairs virtually due to the fact they have got growth the intellectual toughness, many of them sincerely determined themselves and are however rediscovering themselves due to one component and this is "intellectual toughness" as an example, in sports activities activities of football, one man stands proud and that is Christiano Ronaldo, from his Portuguese membership fc Porto to Manchester United and to Real Madrid and now Juventus, he has been doing one trouble and that is "non-forestall schooling after training, and he has a passion for scoring lots of goals, he has a prevailing mentality, he doesn't believe there may be any other player higher than him, even at his pinnacle, he feels he's just starting.

He disciplined the way he eats, he doesn't clearly consume any engaging meals, he eats what is going to preserve him healthful and in shape. Of path, we have had exclusive extremely good game enthusiasts who might have been better than him, however the troubles that they had changed into incapacity to stay regular at what they do for a long term. And that is truely the distinction among Christiano Ronaldo and others.

Mental durability therefore is all encompassing, there's no person path to being mentally hard, you need to should do advantageous subjects that others aren't doing, you want to want to suppose the manner others aren't thinking and you need to ought to preserve a way of existence that is alien to others, only even as this is finished, you could see a trade that is similar to a success people, I'll show you the severa attributes a top notch way to make you stand out maximum of the crowd, your lifestyles will in no manner be the equal if you exercise what I'll show you as you look at on.

As a student you're supply your problem define, you recognize what to examine and take a look at in university, now, it's miles very common that no longer all of the college students usually pass exam, at the same time as some skip the tests in flying colorings, now not all do skip in flying colours, whilst some are common not all are also common, some get A, B, C, D, E or F, the query is how come a number of the student were given "A" this is an tremendous end result, at the equal time as some fall into exclusive training, it didn't simply display up with the useful resource of using danger, ask your self the question, what did the scholars who scored "A" try this others did no longer do. There should be some issue within the lower back of it. After all, all of the university students were given the same curriculum and are doing the identical course, so why did that came about.

It all boils all the manner all of the manner all the way down to one element, and that is highbrow durability. The university university students that rating "A" grade really preferred it and that they had been given it, they did what it takes to get it and this is why they have been given it, if you attempted to get it but fall brief of it, it way you did no longer sincerely do as an entire lot as they did to accumulate it.

But it is virtually conceivable, take a look at them carefully and do extra the following semester to triumph over them or identical their toes. Again it's although relies upon on your degree of "intellectual durability". If you are not mentally hard you can not be able to be a part of up with their performance.

Application of highbrow longevity in technology

Most scientists stand out in their career than others virtually because of the reality they have got a diehard mentality that is very hard at discovering some detail new. A scientist who isn't always inquisitive about coming across a few element new will typically want to rely on what's already contemporary, but the one who's stimulated and spirited will continuously preference to invent a few aspect, he dreams some component new to provide to the arena, some issue that no individual has ever done.

From statistics, we've got were given visible scientist who gave us what we are although the usage of nowadays, collectively with, the precept of developing the LED globe and energy. Michael Faraday the person who positioned strength based totally on a selected principle of electricity he positioned out via private discovery, Thomas Edison, the person who determined the electrical bulb tried severa times and failed however he by no means gave up and he ended up giving the sector one of the finest discoveries of man which precept is in recent times the premise of LED electric powered powered bulb manufacturing. Again, one detail this is common among those guys became mental power, if Thomas Edison gave up his idea on electric powered bulb, then he would likely in no manner have decided it. Mental durability is the potential to constantly stick with what you consider that is going to artwork based totally totally on experimenting in relation to medical discovery.

Many scientists maintain to check on some factor until they see that it is going to work, if it doesn't paintings, they keep on attempting until subsequently they get the result. At this degree, this is the scientists' intellectual toughness, the trust inside the brilliant stop end result of the very last outcomes of what they're inventing. We also can borrow the expertise of the technological knowledge manner of wondering or mentality to growth the location of existence which we placed is close to now not feasible to advantage, I'll rather consider that it's miles going to paintings, and I'll preserve strolling at it till I get it proper.

The first-class factor that makes it not working for now might be clearly due to the fact you have not gotten it proper, and the nice manner you'll ever get it proper is while you maintain walking it and keep on practicing and doing it till you get it right.

The story of Thomas Edison can be very thrilling, he stored on believing that his invention will artwork, he in no manner doubted himself, at the difficulty of giving up, he genuinely observed what have come to be lacking and at the same time as he did located it, the relaxation is records, he were given it right at that 2d, the pain and suffering over the failed attempts become forgotten and what he acquire come to be what no man ever did gain, these days Thomas Edison is one of the famend scientist for his actual works of discovering the electric bulb.

The distinction is that the ones men persisted continuously believing that what they are doing will art work and it did paintings. You will no longer truly believe but upload what you are doing to what you take delivery of as actual with. With the right consider system that 'it's far going to paintings' and in fact doing what you accept as proper with is what's going to provide you with the give up result not even as you don't trust in what you're doing, an first rate way to now not provide you with the right quit give up end result.

Again a man stated inside the course of the time of Aristotle, the awesome Greek philosopher, that guy can not fly, Aristotle opined as an opportunity that man will fly, he believed in what he said, but many human beings mocked him and in response they stated to him "You need to understand that you are incorrect, even the ostrich with wings can't fly, why need to you ever conceive in your mind that man without wings will fly?" and so no person consider what he stated.

But a few years later, guy is flying from america of the united states to u . S . A . From one continent to the possibility and from earth to the moon and outer region. Actually individuals who typically accept as authentic with have a higher intellectual strength or sturdiness than others.

Mental durability also has to do with what you consider, in case you believe in a few aspect and you growth a passion for it, you figure in the direction of accomplishing it, you'll truely get that element. For this has been the tale of many human beings in time past.

Mental durability in the Religious circle

From the spiritual mindset, an act of believing is generally terrific, and I advocate that there's no manner you may have intellectual sturdiness with out believing in what you're doing, due to the fact in case you want fulfillment in any organisation you may should undergo in thoughts in what you're doing. In religious accept as true with as an example, if you need some factor extra normal to occur, you want to wish for it and also have religion, consequently faith is all approximately having the belief, self assurance that what you are praying for will come to fruition. In particular terms, your degree of religion or perception will decide the very last effects of what you are praying for.

In the bible for instance, whilst Jesus healed the blind man, there can be a query he asked it is "do you believe that the son of Man can be able to heal you?" and the blind thoughts answered "show me and I'll trust" and after he changed into healed through Jesus, he asked him to move and inform no person approximately it.

Hence, to belief in some aspect is a precursor to accomplishing what you are walking at or dreaming about, in case you are a student and you want to come to be a clinical physician or a scientist or undertaking into every other profession, the number one detail you want to do is to accept as true with that you can truly comprehend your desires, after this, each special detail you want to do follows it.

We also can talk about the highbrow durability in religion with the problem of the girl with the problem of blood who've been bleeding for twelve years, she super had one conviction based totally on her faith, and he or she or he or he believed that if she may be able to contact the draw close's garments she can be healed. In the midst of the group at the same time as she attempted to try this, she in truth completed it, and right away she touched His dress, Jesus Christ determined that power had flown out from His frame to heal the girl. He absolutely stopped and requested "who touched me?" His disciples have been surprised due to the fact they had been all in the midst of the crowed every person ought to have touched him, so one of the disciples stated to him "draw close it's feasible all and sundry need to have touched you within the midst of the crowed" but He replied "no, it turn out to be one-of-a-type, as soon because the character touched me, energy flew out of me", the female noticing she have end up healed, knew she became the only that grow to be being mentioned and she or he quick submitted herself.

So, in case you don't receive as right with you don't have the intellectual sturdiness, begin believing and you may accumulate that immoderate degree of intellectual sturdiness so that you can make you to stay to tell the story in any of your chosen place in lifestyles.

Why we have got got such a whole lot of not unusual people within the worldwide these days is genuinely due to the level of character's highbrow durability.

I even have seen hundreds of human beings with great ability and competencies to grow to be superstars, however due to low stage of highbrow toughness, they have got not been able to forge in advance in life.

Mental durability therefore is a few aspect this is very crucial and desires urgent interest. Whatever you do as an character, to attain success with it, you need to grow to be mentally tough.

Chapter 2: A Psychologist's Guide to Becoming Psychologically Strong

From the previous economic smash, I delivered to your statistics the which means of Mental toughness from precise point of view and angle. In this chapter I will be taking you via a more scientific methodological method to intellectual sturdiness that is capability and may be carried out in normal existence. It is quite clean to reap, but there are some certain things you can want to do as an character for you a great manner to turn out to be more dominant and get the whole benefits of being mentally strong or difficult.

I generally advice people approximately intellectual sturdiness, it's no longer approximately you on my own, mental sturdiness also has to do together with your functionality to determine, self discovery, information your most powerful factors and developing it, understanding your susceptible factor and improving on it and furthermore having an issue in opposition in your competition or contemporaries. It has to do collectively along with your will to increase your self, to go the more mile in other to fulfill your desires.

Note that it is feasible to look at many books that has to do with private development, but if there can be no will or zeal to use what you've got red from the books, you will by no means make a headway, it's miles a unique component to take a look at approximately private development and it's miles any other thing to the usage of it.

Sometimes to allow an person benefit fulfillment or dream, it may take the efforts of others in what I call "the collective duty for an character's improvement". From this attitude, it takes a teacher or organization of teachers who're schooling in a university to prepare college college college students who are going to turn out to be a fulfillment of their studies, it additionally takes a business commercial enterprise company train to help someone to increase and emerge as a success in commercial enterprise organization, and this is why you'll meet masses of folks who look up to other humans as their mentor or business organization partners or advisors.

In sports sports, you'll furthermore discover that quite a few coaches or managers of agencies have unique psychological strolling footwear or advisors who see to the intellectual energy and improvement of the crew, this can allow the group to simply accept as genuine with in their talents and play to their highest potentials. The obligation of the psychologist is to help assemble the crew or human beings to play to their capability or potentials, to agree with they're better than their combatants usually. In this regard consequently, in some thing you do you want to apply this method of mental improvement which allows you to broaden in the ambient of your potentials step by step and get to the peak of achievement.

Psychologists superior the maximum feasible manner of task fulfillment loads greater with out trouble without having to undergo rigorous sports as a way to will allow you to build in your present herbal highbrow power. I am awesome it is some factor that you may additionally examine within your capability to reap success.

In this determination, I installation the maximum practical approach to what can be received correctly, but, I need to assist you to understand additionally that, in all activities, it is the quantity of efforts which you set up on the way to determine yours achievement, what am I speaking approximately proper here? I endorse in case you need some aspect more than each one of a kind person, and you make a decision to do what it takes to be the first-class, if your quality is certainly the outstanding of the extremely good, of path you may honestly win, however if your tremendous isn't the splendid of the satisfactory, then anticipate a person else who without a doubt worked better at being the incredible of the incredible to choose the coveted fee.

In a nutshell then, I'll want to ask you a few questions which is probably; do you virtually assume you could pass the extra mile at attaining some component great? Do you actually need to conquer all of us who's your fellow competitor? Do you watched you could win even supposing others are competiting with you? What do you reflect onconsideration on your degree of highbrow strength presently and inside the next coming weeks?

If you could discover solutions to this questions, then, I keep in mind in you, I perception you may become what you want to be, I consider you are unstoppable, however if I believe in you and you don't be given as genuine with in yourself, you don't allow me down, you could permit you to down. That is without a doubt the primary trouble, to truely accept as real with in yourself is what is going to propel you to victory, and to consider in yourself is what is going to make you to become the massive in your area of have a study.

I really have watched the overdue Michael Jackson at some point of his younger and person years, I determined one problem approximately him, he doesn't preserve in thoughts there is any of his identical, he surely be what he is, he changed into truely Michael Jackson the entertainer, from his youngsters, he is aware of not some thing other than track, he lived the lifestyles of an entertainer from formative years, his know-how have grow to be placed and advanced and the strength of his intellectual sturdiness modified into amazing.

He sincerely doesn't take transport of failure, he modified into achievement epitomize, why? Because he stood with the resource of and did what he knew a way to do outstanding, he believed lots in it and he have turn out to be what he really have end up ultimately he wrote his very very own facts inside the worldwide. The song enterprise will not be complete without his tale, Guinness books of records may be incomplete without his name, and worldwide awards will no longer be entire with out his name the numerous nice legend of tune that ever lived.

How did this guy achieve success? How did he have become a very big awesome movie famous person on earth, it takes someone with the right highbrow sturdiness to reap this shape of toes, no feebly mental man or woman or willing highbrow person can obtain what the humans that belong to the highbrow durability group can gather the volume of fulfillment. This is surely the distinction.

From the foregoing, you could study and agree that the essential problem we've were given inside the global nowadays as a long manner as human beings are worried is that humans do not have get right of access to to psychologist who can be capable to take care of the intellectual durability, in real truth many do now not recognize that they've a problem of being now not being mentally difficult, and this is why we are capable of hold to have those who adore and characteristic a laugh well-known folks who without a doubt have the intellectual sturdiness to excel in their decided on careers. Have you ever requested your self, what's so unique about sports activities sports women and men, actors and actresses, song artists and different celebrities and famous people, why is it that the media communicate a lot approximately them and their lifestyle, why is it that they are making all of the coins this is very huge within the place wherein they've got pitched their profession?

It all boils right down to one element and this is "their highbrow sturdiness has been exploited to their non-public gain"

I strongly take delivery of as real with that if each person within the worldwide that we live in are mentally tough, lots of them is probably a success, I'm no longer bragging about this, it's far what I actually have almost visible take location in real life. There isn't whatever which could stop an character from succeeding in existence with the proper highbrow durability.

Mental sturdiness therefore comes with a fee and there are certain characteristics which might be typically associated with humans who've intellectual longevity. This can be mentioned in subsequent chapters as we have a take a look at on.

Therefore, if you are reading this e-book, you want to additionally recall yourself very fortunate that you have found the proper additives, just like I stated, mental durability is run to many those who later emerge as famous each they're in a selected area or profession, take as an example, sports sports men and women who have get right of get admission to to to wearing centers and a psychologist who works on their intellectual sturdiness to ensure they maximize their capacity, this is the gain the ones sports activities sports men and women have over normal folks which can be hired in a organization.

Many corporations don't see the want to get a psychologist to help teach the intellectual sturdiness of their personnel, and so they hold on final on the nation that they were employed. Although a few companies or businesses can also decide to carry out regular in-residence training, seminar and workshop for their personnel, but no longer all of them do this.

The education via a number of those companies serves as a moral or intellectual booster. Sometimes the favored outcomes may be performed however at the equal time because the worker leaves the employment it certainly ends there.

The improvement is extra rapid and quicker with sports activities ladies and men who are constantly receiving steady training and take part in competitions, they have get right of entry to to psychologist who's an expert in the difficulty of getting prepared them earlier of tournaments and club or u . S . A . Engagements. This is what makes the distinction, that is what cause them to to become one of the most paid or earnings earners amongst people. Now this truth has demonstrated that to get a teacher for your mental durability, you'll need to move the greater mile.

Firstly, in case you need to get a psychologist who will assist in building your intellectual sturdiness, you can want to have the coins to have enough money his offerings. And in case you are not able to pay his or her fee, then you may now not get get admission to to a psychologist who is probably able to help your state of affairs.

One of the reasons that made me to take a company desire in penning this ebook is because I absolutely have the interest of human beings internal your beauty at heart due to the reality I actually need to help many humans rediscover themselves and turn out to be mentally difficult.

By the time you are completed with the content material fabric material of this book, you may get big rate for your money because of the truth, you will be demonstrated what it takes to be mentally tough and as you can see already, you've got grow to be extra in song with the statistics in this ebook.

This e-book is probably a supply of reference for a few component that has to do with intellectual durability, take it up and take a look at on the same time as you workout what you look at and apply it to your each day existence, it's far very critical to apprehend that, even as you get a replica of this book, you will be relaxation confident that during case you can't pay a psychologist, this ebook has already finished the manner in your ethical and highbrow boosting, you can constantly come another time to have a observe the components that has to do collectively along with your mental development as you still struggle for survival.

Today, a whole lot of humans need the services of a psychologist, however they may in no way acquire that they do, but in actual truth, the position of a psychologist cannot be overvalued, why due to the fact we've had been given visible how they were capable of deal with so many troubles that has to do with man or woman's underperformances and the way they've got helped in building them to emerge as exquisite humans.

As all of us preserve to stay each day inside the worldwide, we're certain to face many stressful situations, some of this worrying conditions can only be handled if we've the highbrow durability, that is why we pay attention statements like "taking the bull by using the use of manner of the horn" all of us will need to stand it either we like it or no longer, there will generally be a time at the same time as you could want to face reality and you may need to arise to the take a look at.

If you don't have the highbrow sturdiness, you can without a doubt fizzle out, whether or not it's far company, education, non-public business company or circle of relatives or possibly in governance, if you aren't mentally hard, don't be amazed you'll fizzle out or out of area out in the race. If you're in an area of role, a person is looking and planning to take over that function from you, if you are in a feature of authority, someone someplace may simply be scheming and planning your downfall in order that she or he can be capable of take that function from you. It happens all of the time.

You were strolling in a business enterprise for the beyond 5 to ten years, you've not gotten any selling, and a person somewhere is sitting on your merchandising. That's how depraved some agency organisation may be, what will you do if you face challenges? Do you experience depressed and give up otherwise you combat and live robust to mention what is rightfully yours? Whatever you are questioning remains has to do alongside aspect your intellectual electricity and durability, in case you are vulnerable mentally, there can be no way you can live to tell the story the maneuvering of some men or women in a corporation company who're so determined for energy.

In the conditions, you could take delivery of as proper with me that each living person in this global desires a psychologist who will help him or her to increase intellectual sturdiness, the most important motive why human beings fail to gather their reason is due to the reality they do now not have highbrow sturdiness, that you fail doesn't recommend that you can not make it in some factor you're in search of to gain. No! Is truly because of the fact you gave up while you can clearly attempt to enhance to reap that trouble. Secondly, there are techniques to achieving your desires, a course that desires to be found, the manner that leads to success, is in reality which you did not have a observe that direction or take the right step inside the right course.

You actually need a psychologist's manual if you locate it hard to compete together along with your contemporaries, life itself is a opposition, learning the manner to stay to tell the tale is viable, however surviving well could be very critical. Don't surely exist with out surviving, you may be modern and but you are not surviving.

For instance, if you have $1,000 for your monetary organization account and a hassle of $50,000 comes your way, surely you're in hassle, because your $1,000 can not address the $50,000 problem. Do you presently see?

But if you have a trouble of $one hundred,000 and you've $20,000,000 to your monetary institution account, that hassle is solved in advance than its starts offevolved or ends.

You need to have a observe yourself and understand why the pinnacle earners within the worldwide keep to make extra cash, on the same time as the little profits earners, emerge as spending and not having sufficient. Is not a mistake, it's in fact because of the reality the top earners within the worldwide these days have extend their intellectual sturdiness and tailor-made it inside the route of undertaking fulfillment and the results is having an increasing number of earnings which continues to generate greater coins and they will be able to make investments and earn extraordinarily getting to some extent of turning into financially loose.

These top earners within the international nowadays did now not in fact end up superstars over night, it took them someday, through schooling and private development they were capable of boom the mind-set of staying mentally tough, they became recognition and comprehend what they want and that they worked towards it and subsequently finished what they desired.

The psychologist guide therefore is some thing that everyone wishes, and I will inspire you to constantly refer once more to this ebook to hold you on the track if you ever encounter any hassle, this grasp piece is the tonic you need to get decrease again on course.

I as soon as met a younger guy who end up feeling depressed, what befell to him turn out to be that during his first 12 months in the University, at the same time as he have been given admission, he started out out attending lectures but determined it tough to have a look at via or recognize the route, a few subjects have been tough for him to recognize, he approached a number of his instructors, and desired solution, but first-rate few of them need to help, pretty a number of them had been very busy and wouldn't have the time with him. So he felt dejected and step by step have become depressed. His intellectual reputation have grow to be prone and in advance than he positioned out it, the examination preparations become very terrible and he didn't do properly, he failed about four guides out of the twelve and he best controlled to skip final eight.

While I discovered his countenance, I approached him and he shared his trouble with me, I desired to assist him get decrease returned heading in the proper path, I told him a few aspect that's what I commenced out with in this e-book, and this is "to accept as true with" he had out of area faith in himself, but I recommended him I believe he can pass the ones courses, I informed him he can emerge as a higher lecturer inside the ones courses he failed, that captivated his hobby and he had been given interested in the communique, he desired to understand extra, due to the fact I touched the sensitive a part of his thoughts this is his intellectual power, he come to be though a scholar, and in that times I had to determine out a way to reach his brains. I stated something that added on his mind and he got the booster he wanted, he believed due to the reality I believed in him, I believed that he need to do it and he were given inspired due to the truth I believed he ought to do it.

That second we chatted grew to end up round to come to be a 2nd of trade in his life and he were given up and thanked me very a whole lot, I gave him a boost, I were given him lower lower back on path while he wondered away, many people in the international are just like that.

Why do you located many human beings commit suicide? Is no difference, they may find out frustration inside the "hand of life", they weren't looking forward to their existence will turn out to be what it is now and that they give up all hopes, in the end, because of the fact there may be no man or woman to help them decrease returned on target, they turn out to be in melancholy, self pity and the frustration is an excessive amount of for them to deal with, then, the subsequent trouble they do is committing suicide. This guide is the primary change mantra with the intention to exchange your life, alternate your mindset and boom you right into a mentally tough character that you want to be to emerge as that incredible person you ought to be.

Chapter 3: Develop Resilience

Before I flow in addition to talk approximately being resilient, I need you to take a deep breath and assume internal yourself; ask yourself the query approximately resilience, what does it take to be resilience? Am I resilient? What makes you placed which you are resilient?

Let me begin through discussing about what it way to be resilience.

What is Resilience

From the definition given with the aid of Merriam Webster's collegiate dictionary, Resilience is the functionality of a strained body to get higher its length and form after deformation due to whole strain, secondly, it's miles an ability to recover from or alter effortlessly to misfortune or alternate, being capable of recover from surprise with out being completely deformed.

One of the number one issue that has saved a achievement and well-known human beings going, is their degree of resilience, whether or not or no longer it is sports, organisation, training, era and in all location of life, the simplest component that generally differentiates successful human beings from the most opposed industrial employer surroundings or competitive environment is their unusual highbrow toughness to be successful, I've seen situations whilst folks who are thriving to achieve a very difficult situation out of place their functionality to stay resilient regardless of the difficult scenario they may be dealing with, maximum of them emerge as giving up on their desires and in addition they fizzle out or change surroundings to a few special locations. Why is it so, it's actually because they have got no longer normal a way of closing resolute in their quest for survival.

If you must be resilient you have to make up your thoughts no longer to give up on tough situations, you need to stand corporation regardless of what takes region to you. You ought to stay interest at the final result. Most a fulfillment humans inside the global in recent times did now not just benefit success in inside the destiny, in actual fact, a hit humans commonly go through an extended journey in advance than they arrive, and there are various levels of sports activities that they undergo. Most times is what they conceive of their minds, and that is in which it all starts offevolved, they idea of some problem, they belief over it over a while body, they began seeing the opportunity of bringing it to existence, they begin the technique, from one approach to each different, in generation, it's miles concept, data, hypothesis, method, test, idea and surrender.

These sports are geared towards knowing some thing and bringing it to existence and if it does exercise, then it becomes a generally awesome phenomenon. Therefore, you need to recognize that a success humans commonly undergo a few ranges and sports activities that truely shape their future, take for instance individuals who are into sports activities sports sports. They commonly sign up in a unmarried academy or the opposite, and the basics of the sports is being perception, folks who get the vision will fast begin the processing of their brains and it step by step settles down into them. The information and the nifty gritty of the sports sports sports are uncovered to them, the coaches or running shoes start to discover the talents and that is it, and the individual involved captures and develops it inside the brain.

The approach starts with know-how and having the possibility to be exposed to the trainings in case you want to make you've got the mind that you certainly ought to hold on doing what you are doing, and that may not come clean due to the fact in each component of the video video games there may be continually rigorous or normal trainings, the trainings completed is to will let you compete in hard situations, the rudiment of the sports activities sports sports activities sports is positioned thru to you and also you want to go through it inside the palms of those people who are out to make you recognize it.

Sometimes the ones sports dreams sacrifice and region, you may want to remain notable and keep on going, following the basics and are aware of it.

In every of the sports activities, there are continuously policies and policies, you'll want to stay and hold to it in any other case you'll lose touch of the complete idea. Being resilient means that; you need to recognize and make bigger the thoughts-set that will help you to live in touch with the purpose of the path.

It goals pretty a few sacrifice close to being resilient, many people surrender with out problem once they fail on the quest of something, counting on the location, in case you fail an examination for instance otherwise you failed an interview for instance, you shouldn't experience that it's the end of the area. No! You need to pick out out up yourself and preserve, try again, hold trying and artwork hard to pass it the following time, which you fail on your first strive doesn't imply you may no longer bypass the subsequent one.

Failure is quality a Postponed success

If you are doing commercial enterprise organization and you've got got did now not establish your logo, and your business enterprise is sprucing off, don't lose preference, because you first-class observed one manner of accomplishing fulfillment, sure! That is the manner I term it, even as you fail in organization, recognize that others moreover failed in their attempts, if you do a studies you'll discover that many people who started out out out enterprise surely were given their fingers burnt, they fail of their first strive at getting the enterprise taking walks. So don't give up, you want to get better and get it going. That you fail in a single specific company doesn't advise you may not attain a few different industrial business agency.

If you are schooling and also you don't get to bypass your examination, don't fear, in case you fail, hello! Failure is simplest a postpone success, test the statistics of the guy who scored the very high-quality mark, take a look at his or her result and say to it, if that is what a person did, I can score a better mark, start running toward it and achieve it, beat it, be the boy or female to overcome, stand out, you are the excellent at what you do, if you don't be the great no person will permit you to be the wonderful except the only who's helping you to get there as your mentor.

The capability to accumulate surprise or disappointments

Before you'll be a resilient character, it begins together together with your attitude, at the same time as your mind is ready already, you may be able to get keep of something involves you. To be that difficult minded individual, it takes quite some education and the orientation you get will determine how a long way you may be able to go. Your orientation subjects because of the reality besides you get the right orientation, you may now not make it to enhance in highbrow sturdiness.

Being resilient may be examined even as you got a shock from what is going on around you, if you have been forced up already and a person is trying to frustrate you the extra, and you do not care and however believe you can overcome any obstacle area earlier than you; then you can get hold of as actual with that you are mentally sturdy. People go through hard instances, when such a person gets into tough state of affairs that has an inclination to break him or her, the man or woman doesn't give up and keep a excessive degree of optimism and finds answers to the trouble that individual has a robust mentality.

You are hit through some element that has a tendency to weaken you, some thing which can make you cry, a few factor that would make you sense the complete international is crashing, but you're capable of stand your ground and face the hassle and truly obliterate or take manipulate of the state of affairs, this means that you're mentally robust.

If you get right into a situation which could devastate you and you're able to stress your manner decrease back heading in the right direction at the identical time as you skip on collectively along with your every day interest with out feeling terrible approximately the situation, you are in the proper nation of being resilient. Resilient is a few difficulty that maintains you coming lower returned after a fall or misfortune. When a few humans meet misfortune in their lives they'll not hold with their ordinary sports sports, they have a tendency to be outcomes dissatisfied at the same time as such topics show up.

That method that individual is not resilient, however if there can be some thing that happens to a person and the man or woman maintains on moving, the individual is unfazed with the useful resource of what occurs to her or him, that person is resilient.

I certainly have watched a football in shape someday in 1989 held in one of the Asian countries it changed into a totally tough healthy at some stage inside the semi final of the FIFA underage opposition, the under 21 international cup, at half of of of time one of the crew became 4 nil down. At the resumption of the second one half, the psychologist's approach changed into employed on the loosing organization; they had been being endorsed that they have got the potential of coming returned into the sport. And when they were given to the second 1/2 of, they finished and pretty much fifteen minutes to the surrender of the in form the desires started coming in, through the ninetieth minute 3 desires had been replied again and at 90 minutes, there has been an equalizer. From four dreams down within the first half of and pretty a terrific deal fifteen minutes to the stop of the healthful a miracle had taken region, the in shape ended up in effects and the group who believed hundreds in themselves who stayed strong and resilient were given the victory on the surrender of the more time. Why did this display up? Is none aside from resilience, if the loosing organization gave up the combat before the surrender of the second one half of as most corporation do, they wouldn't have advantage such feet. Even if whilst one of the athletes have been given injured, the group despite the fact that went ahead and received the in shape, it become a pyrrhic victory, and that during form stays being stated hitherto.

Resilience is one characteristic that an character should make crucial efforts at inculcating due to the fact your capacity to be resilient will help in supplying you with success each time the immediate comes.

Again each other instance is one well-known American wrestler referred to as Shawn Michaels, he changed into later nick named the Heart Break Kid, why? Because he became a splendid example of a resilient athlete, Shawn will input the ring with a whole lot of self guarantee towards his combatants, he wasn't a large man, he end up commonplace however with a massive coronary heart, Shawn have become recognised for his ability to transport a completely lengthy distance collectively along with his combatants, even though Shawn's opponent have been typically massive in period, Shawn may get preserve of a beating for numerous minutes or hours but but his opponent will no longer be able to pin him, Shawn's resilience typically weakens his opponents, he have end up wonderful at frustrating his fighters after which at the stop the warring parties will tire out and Shawn will take benefit and inflict a defeat on his opponent. This became how Shawn have come to be a expert in being resilient, and he were given the recognition as the "coronary coronary heart destroy child" due to the reality he end up capable of cause numerous disillusioned on his unsuspected opponents who had concept he could be smooth to conquer. He have become definitely an average length man, but his resilience have grow to be an indicator, he defeated many huge wrestlers.

Your resilience will generally make you to defeat your situation and activities, receive as proper with it. Learn to be resilient; I'll give you the tale of a piece canine and a larger canine. Once upon a time, there has been this small canine which typically leaves his little house and is going to satisfy a larger dog inside the neighboring residence and start barking at it. The large canine will pop out and beat it up and the smaller dog will run away lower again to its little house, the next day the little canine will bypass lower back and start a fight, the massive dog comes out to triumph over it up and the small dog will pass once more domestic, tomorrow the small dog comes out to start a combat, it went on like that each day till the larger dog became bored to death in the small canine, the big dog left his residence for the small dog and in no way came once more.

That is the energy of resilience, do not forget the definition of resilience, being capable of face up to impediment without being surely devastated. The little canine definitely desired to take over the house of the massive canine, and it used its very own intellectual sturdiness, its private intellectual toughness in the direction of that of the massive canine and the small canine won the conflict regardless of the range of times it were given crushed and overpowered at some level within the every day fights. The small dog had a reason, it remained centered on achieving its goal and desires, and it did not prevent harassing the big dog until it had been given what it preferred.

You can be passing thru tough moments, subjects won't be operating nicely for you, however live recognition and preserve to paintings tough to exchange that scenario, take the bull thru manner of the horn, similar to the small canine, it took the massive canine on a completely lengthy journey, the use of its private resilience, the small canine grow to be in a feature to break the huge dog's length into small quantities, surely due to its resilience.

So, some thing you do in existence, be resilient, in case you are a student and you are attempting difficult to bypass your assessments and you failed in multiple strive, what you need to do is to begin analyzing hard and put together better, burn the mid night time time candle, be regular and persistent along side your look at, on the same time as others are gambling and dropping their valuable times on subjects for you to no longer add fee to their research. You can chose to visit the library to check greater, have a look at greater hard and beautify on yourself; these are sports activities that display resilience in schooling.

If you are a businessman or woman, you have had been given issues taking your organization to the next degree, don't get discourage, all you need is to re-strategize, take some time to appearance inward, find out in which your commercial company is not doing nicely and beautify on it, take the essential movement to reinforce that vicinity of your organisation that is inclined, if it is a few element that has to do with advertising, workout your fee variety, if it's miles getting the proper professionals into positions with a purpose to make the most their abilties for the benefit or growth of the enterprise, get the proper specialists to address the activity, if it is the vicinity that desires the right candidate or employees to fill vacant positions, get them to paintings and determine what to do with them to make your employer expand faster.

Work out your budget to run your enterprise, many company businesses get into troubles related to tax and overhead value, floating a organization every now and then may be very cumbersome, the early stages of business business enterprise organization is regularly marred with wonderful challenges, a few commercial agency start small and they bypass regularly, others begin massive and soon come crashing and come to be finishing. Most businesses start small and follow the showed strategies to develop massive.

Most individuals that lead organization revolution or improvement are absolutely people with better intellectual durability, once they gift their proposals to banks, they're able to get the important begin up capitals due to the fact the banks may additionally furthermore see thru their intellectual electricity their potential to deliver while given the loans. Most instances those people with intellectual durability have already set up business employer that is already doing well, they get credit score for that and the bank keep in mind their resilience at succeeding and that they frequently get loans to boom their organizations.

The thriller of being resilient

One of the pinnacle mystery whilst a person is resilient is the fact that resilience will usually motive fulfillment, because of the fact the greater you preserve strolling at a few problem, the more you preserve doing that detail, you hold education it, you hold on appearing that problem, you get the very satisfactory hazard of engaging in perfection at what you are doing.

Study distinctive mother and father which may be Resilient

You want to start analyzing unique parents which is probably resilient, you'll be capable of recognize how this humans are making subjects show up with their potential to come to be resilient at what they may be doing, we have got a number of people who've grow to be legend due to their being resilient, regardless of what assignment in advance than you, you have got the ability to succeed and end up a success, at the same time as you observe others, you'll be able to determine their electricity and the manner their story started and the way they were capable of collect or what they have carried out to date as they've got end up very resilient.

Be Patient

Don't be in a rush to get some thing that you are looking for, am now not saying you must prevent but as an alternative, exercise subjects strategically with examined techniques as hired in this ebook, you've heard from the antique saying that the affected person dog will consume the fattest bone, why? Due to the truth while different puppies had been fighting for the bone, they fought every superb and forgot the bone, and on the identical time as they had been busy combating the affected man or woman canine in reality walked in and took the bone away, if the later joined inside the fight, it's going to in no manner get the bone, some different dog will come and take it away, however on the same time as the alternative dogs were fighting, the affected individual dog surely deliberate and strategized, searching the alternative puppies fighting and forgetting the bones and it genuinely went and took the big bone and left.

Think about it, something you're seeking out in existence, you need to devise and take a superb technique that others aren't taking. There is constantly one way to wearing out fulfillment and whilst you comply with it you will get there.

Patience consequently is one trends of someone who is mentally hard, you will be conscious that they continuously plan in advance in any of their sports sports that they worried themselves in. Being affected person will allow you to peer via matters very surely and what desire is to be taken when confronted with stiff stressful conditions.

Be awareness in knowing your dream

A lot of humans honestly lose cognizance and without issue get distracted away from getting to the aspect of success; that is in which I am going to make you recognize that being attention is a manner of enhancing to your highbrow durability. Let me percentage from the well-known revel in of 1 athlete within the track and location. He is a house keep call, an Olympic champion through benefit, he has been examined and depended on and he has been placed via screening and he doesn't have any issues with drug cheating, he in no manner used drug enhancing basic performance to excel in his state of affairs. His name is Husain Bolt, this man broke his very personal document at the Olympics and these days he stands tall among his pairs, while he modified into interviewed he replied and stated "on every occasion he starts offevolved a race his interest is on the gold medal".

He categorically stated that "every time the sound of the whistle is blown and the race begins offevolved, he doesn't care approximately who or what his competition are, all that is in his thoughts at that moment is the gold medal", in some manner, that has labored for him over time, he is seemed for his multiple gold medal triumphing streaks all through his debut in the Olympic games.

That is the mind of a champion; a champion doesn't receives distracted through the satisfactory of his fellow competitors or contemporaries inside the industrial agency.

Husain has through the years keep a wholesome level of attention and that has really worked for him. If you're into something that has to do with super productivity, usually attempt your possible first-rate to be centered.

What does it take to be targeted?

To remain focused is to live in latest concentration inside the route of the aim which you purchased all the way down to benefit without permitting yourself to be distracted with what's taking place to your surroundings.

It doesn't depend wide variety what all people says about what you are making plans to do or what you are doing to gain achievement, being resilient is what topics because in case you achieve success you will be the only an great manner to be affected and celebrated if making a decision to fail you are though going to get mocked at. So why don't you are taking the proper preference through staying attention for your dreams so that you can achieve it. You need to passionately pursue your desires through staying interest.

Focus inside the vicinity of technological know-how constantly refers to a specific spot, in physics as an instance, at the same time as we communicate about interest, we speakme approximately the issue in which there may be a convergence or cognizance. But however, in actual existence situation we are nearly reasoning alongside the same line with the scientist, that specialize in a specific reason that want to be or can be finished is what makes us to have the intellectual capability and durability to attain it. Especially, whilst we are residing in a cutting-edge society wherein there may be opposition for vicinity, corporation or to dominate the marketplace. When there may be a prize at stake, we usually have the first characteristic, second function and the 1/three characteristic and others prizes to be received. Everyone will need to compete for the top spot.

Take as an instance the FIFA international cup, that comes up as speedy as in each 4 years, the thirty four agencies that commonly compete constantly need to win the primary prize, each united states of the us wants to increase the FIFA worldwide cup, this is the most important success inside the international of soccer, but the first spot is exceptional for one u.S.. Hence, there may be typically stiff competition; a crew that wants to win want to live recognition.

I honestly have witnessed notable groups who've the potentials of winning the sector cup, however a few aspect will come up within the group, either one participant is having troubles with the teach or a group having hassle with the National handlers, they usually have a tendency to search for their demands, which may be disagreements on bonuses to be paid to the game enthusiasts or allowances, this can motive a vital disunity within the crew. The team in the long run out of place attention and will never play to its capability, thereby getting eliminated in the early tiers of the competition.

Being hobby is inevitable as it will assist you to remain within the path of the organization's quest to win the competition. So additionally it is in actual lifestyles state of affairs, in case you out of place awareness on what you desire to reap with what you are doing, you will omit the mark of achievement and get on the incorrect issue of life, and such is the case related to folks who lose recognition on what they may be doing.

You will never see someone who has intellectual sturdiness losing interest, due to the fact in the event that they do, they may by no means gain that which makes them to be champions. Again, I'll display you example of a extra youthful guy in the global of soccer whom I perceived and I've studied him for the ultimate decade and I come to end, that to me, he's although the number one player, that is the individual with reference to being recognition. He isn't any other than Lionel Messi of Argentina, I've observed that in each mission, this more youthful man has commonly stay centered, I've watched him performed for FIFA underage competition and collectively alongside with his present club, FC Barcelona, this extra youthful guy has typically been centered, he in no way lets in a minute to skip without staying recognition, exceptional companies who have faced him continually have the lack of capacity to live interest and they regularly get punished thru this extra younger guy, the way he performs, he attaches seriousness to it and that capability to live focused all the time within the path of games has made him to end up an enigma in his chosen profession.

Lionel doesn't alternate his fashion of play, he's despite the fact that the equal antique Messi that every institution inside the La Liga is privy to, how come they have got not been capable of have a have a look at his style of play and decrease his functionality to get beyond them, it's certainly due to one element known as recognition and resilience.

When you're resilient one of a kind group don't want to be very first-rate at preventing you, you're the one so you can determine if you may be stopped or now not, you undergo in thoughts the tale of the small canine, it have come to be constantly doing what it believes will defeat the massive dog and it did acquire its goal. To be awareness therefore is probably capable of decide your intellectual durability. People who're generally targeted at engaging in some thing constantly emerge as attaining what they are looking for. Like the vintage pronouncing "shoot for the sun and you could come to be being the various stars". This is a totally real announcement, you can not high-quality end up being maximum of the stars, you will be the shining moderate or solar if you truly live reputation and resilient.

Focus is all approximately popularity, ask yourself the following query:

How frequently have I stayed focused inside the route of my goals?

Have you ever written down your goals and targeted on it?

Have you ever concept approximately attaining a few aspect tremendous?

Have you concept approximately greatness?

What do you understand approximately the those who are outstanding in this global?

What do you think they've finished to attain greatness?

Is there a way feasible to gain greatness, similar to one of a kind humans inside the international?

If you need to appearance inwards you will discover that there may be a vacuum to your life, and that vacuum desires to be stuffed up. It takes you and a dependable mentor to manual you to reap that intention.

When you live interest, it manner which you have pushed a protracted manner from you all distraction, there may be no longer something everybody will say to you if you want to have an effect on you, you will become like a robust rock that can not be moved from a selected spot to every other, it doesn't do not forget the kind of instances you could have failed for your previous tries, the precept problem is as a way to behave proper in any occasions and on the manner to propel you to victory. In nowadays's international, many humans fade away truly because of the truth there has been no character to provide them a pep speak, nobody to offer them the desired idea to excel in their severa existence endeavors, no individual to assist them stay focused.

Your stage of success is probably determined with the resource of the quantity of attention quotient which you have, whenever the time comes with a purpose to continue to be focused, constantly try as loads as viable to live on top of things of your senses. Whenever there can be a stiff competition, the folks that stay recognition and look at the directives of the coaches or teacher are typically folks that come to be doing properly.

As you observe, I'll love you to take notes of the salient factors which need to do with being recognition, make certain you're able to increase your stage of attention which plays a large role for your quest at engaging in a more potent intellectual improvement.

Now there can be a few element which you want to be privy to, and that is, what do you do while there can be distraction?

I apprehend by way of using the usage of now you might have been thinking as soon as I stated you need to be focused, does it advise you'll in no way get distracted, in no manner, distraction will normally come to you, It's something all of us cannot keep away from, whether or not or not or now not you stay a ways from distraction, undergo in thoughts you aren't a lonely island, regular you may need to have interaction with people spherical you, and as a manner to constantly cause distractions.

If you are schooling or in a business enterprise surroundings, you meet special human beings every day and some thing transpires among you and them comes to the table whilst there can be war. In every human interplay, the chance of getting yourself in a war of words is better and that's why we want to get ourselves abreast with the diverse acts of conversation among severa human beings that cuts in the course of the society and that is what we are making you to recognize. Despite the various interactions that we've, the want to stay and maintain in contact with our maximum crucial purpose may be very crucial.

For you to remain focused in existence you'll need to have positive characteristics which might be:

•Never allow your self to be intimidated through your opponents.

•in no way supply in to distractions

•don't allow extraordinary human beings's achievement get into your head

•your very personal achievement is an lousy lot greater important than others

•no individual is higher than you, you are the exceptional at what you do

•take delivery of as real with the fact that there may be opposition

•remember that you by myself is the first-rate and you want to conquer your own information

•don't permit your beyond reviews to get into your head

•see yourself due to the fact the champion who has received the competition or name already

•your fellow competition aren't better than you

•consider turning into the remaining man reputation

When you start to suppose on this way, there may be every possibility that you could simply win or come near prevailing. This mentality degree of questioning will continuously make you to stay beforehand amongst your pears, because your thinking will propel you to break your personal data, once you are capable of do this, then your degree of recognition has superior and better organized for the following diploma.

Learn from the Mistakes of Others

Being resilient is super whilst you do no longer repeat the equal mistakes others did. When you observe humans who have grow to be a success, you want to additionally recognize or take a look at their important state of affairs, which embody what made them become extra a fulfillment than others and also you moreover need to observe why they failed at a positive element of their lifestyles, and once they did fail, you ask questions to understand in the event that they genuinely did rise once more to former glories, if they did no longer rise from their failure, find out why and what saved them from getting returned to their preceding triumphing tactics.

You can be stunned to find out that maximum a achievement folks who failed had one hassle or the other that triggered their downfall, so if you need to stay in advance and grow to be a higher champion, you need to preserve a certain level of statistics about a success folks who made it huge and fall lower back to oblivion.

Don't provide room for Complacency

Being complacent is a manner of questioning which you have arrived at the high-quality spot on your existence, it's far a time that makes you sense comfortable with what you have got benefit and consequently making a decision to relaxation. This can be very volatile, due to the fact definitely at the equal time as you believe you studied you've got got finished what you're searching out or competing for, a few one in all a kind individuals or institution is honestly following you and are operating needed to overtake you. Therefore if you need to live mentally hard you don't want to provide room for complacency, being resilient is at the same time as you are not complacent, you make a decision now not to relaxation until you bought. Sometimes humans have a propensity to lighten up at the numeral laurels, they will be so contented with what they have, as an example, if an athlete wins a occasion or competition, it occurred due to the fact he or the group organized very well and that they obtained. They won due to the fact their mentality became immoderate, they believed they could win and they played to their maximum capability. But the equal employer comes lower returned in two years time to compete inside the identical competition and that they have got a minnow or underrated team, within the event that they feel that they might without trouble stroll over the underrated group, and then they could as well be plotting their non-public removal.

Teams constantly put together and it's miles feasible with the right intellectual durability any crew in a opposition stands a risk to raise the trophy, so if you want to have intellectual durability you have to not offer room for complacency.

In the corporate global, groups can also start business enterprise and start to develop steadily, because the year roles thru the business agency can document huge achievement and it can be doing well within the market, however on the same time as the income generated isn't always nicely controlled to assist in growing the horizon of the corporation, it can discover itself struggling with any competitor who's higher organized to take over the marketplace.

Constant schooling and studies is being deployed by way of manner of huge and smaller enterprise to make sure they continuously decorate their corporation to maximize earnings, no matter the fulfillment of a enterprise, there need to be no street or giving of room for complacency to negatively have an effect at the financial employer industrial business enterprise company.

In training, while a pupil rest and stop studding, the student may moreover possibly start to neglect what she or he has learnt over the period of his or her training, even as the exam is close by, the self warranty will not be there if such scholar cannot have a look at, consequently there have to be no room for complacency whilst you are present process your academic pursuit. You need to be earlier of the beauty then keep your have a test, you want to be the first-rate student then spend more of some time analyzing and doing research on your study. You need to attain the high-quality grade? You'll need to move the more mile to get the desired consequences.

I surely have moreover determined within the gift global of technological development, organizations involved within the production business business enterprise have been carrying out numerous grades of technological gadget production, some were doing well whilst some of them have fizzle out a number of the top manufacturers. Companies that have fared better typically become a hit due to the reality they'll be capable of vision the triumphing mentality and the right intellectual sturdiness to supersede their competition.

That is why you can see the volumes of amazing merchandise coming from those organizations. Hence, with resilience although commercial enterprise agency is doing well, they stored on believing that it's going to paintings and it did artwork for them, that is the identical form of mentality you need to have as an person or proprietor of a business organisation. Always preserve that you're going to interrupt information, that you're going to make it large and ultimately emerge as a success.

Take word of the following key factors:

- Always consider you are certainly beginning

- Don't expect you have got were given won something even when you have acquired truely

- Don't underestimate your opponent

- don't exchange your perception

- belief that you're going to win

- stay devoted to the path

- see yourself prevailing already in advance than the game starts offevolved offevolved

- attempt as a good deal as you may to interrupt your very very own records

- live united to the game plan

- art work in harmony with the alternative members of the organization

- put off the thoughts of susceptible factor from your mind

- play for your largest potentials

- use what you need to accumulate your dreams

- cooperate with distinct participants of the group

- stay calm and focus on what you need to gather

- do not display symptoms of tiring out

- if you get tired, have a touch rest to recuperate

- continuously plan your moves

- strategize a winning method as a manner to make you a fulfillment

- recognize one of a kind competition however ensure you have got an part over them

•skip the more mile to do what others aren't doing

Non-negotiable Fight Back

After you have got got successfully expand a diploma of discernment, you are step by step building your intellectual sturdiness, and it is becoming obvious which you had been putting in region your self and organized to beautify. One subjects comes your way and this is unexpected surprise, how difficult are you to get maintain of sock, don't forget to be resilient, you want as a way to accumulate surprise and also you have to be capable of respond definitely, any scenario or instances that inflicts shock on you, the way you respond to it's going to decide how mentally difficult you are, for example, while you get a lousy information approximately your organisation, maybe your commercial enterprise is ready to crash or suffers a massive loss, how do you respond to such.

When such difficulty takes location to you which ones ones of them can be a misfortune, all you need to do is to actually receive the reality that a few element unfortunate has came about.

If you be given that reality, then the subsequent element you need to be thinking about is a way to get out of these unsightly activities, this is the right step within the right course. I truly have visible a few people after they revel in a misfortune, the way they react is as a substitute horrible, all you be aware them do is begin crying over spilt milk. Crying in no manner solves a problem, rather it in addition aggravates the anxiety surrounding the trouble, crying encourages a kingdom of being hopeless, like there can be no approach to the trouble.

To be resilient in that instances, you want to start stopping once more, irrespective of the problem is, start thru proffering the options you need to bring about the answer to such hassle. Being resilient is what maintain you going and on the equal time as you begin to motive that now not anything can genuinely break you, no longer even your spirit can be broken even as you are resilient. I don't recognize in case you apprehend at the same time as your resilient is so stubborn that your opponent feels threatened via your presence, this I truely have visible happens to many human beings.

So, when you live resolute, it's time so that you can combat decrease decrease returned, you do this thru going via the hassle, begin searching out solution, see it as one of the situation while someone has to rise up and face fact, you could do it and no longer whatever can prevent you from reaching your intention.

The Israelite whilst they were moving out of Egypt, the great exodus, it didn't seem without them coping with disturbing situations, they have been given to a point of no skip back, it changed into the Israelite going thru the purple sea and on the same time being pursued with the beneficial useful resource of Pharaoh's military. That come to be the factor they have been faced with tough scenario and that they've been afraid, some of the humans started out blaming Moses for bringing them into their doom, they started out out to don't forget the existence in Egypt, at that second, they could select out to stay in Egypt in preference to getting their freedom from slavery.

What you need to recognize proper right here is that, at sure element, you get discouraged you start to get the temptation of giving up to your goals, you forget how some distance you have got were given come and also you want to give up the entirety. Remember, the same element came about to the Israelite. But how did Moses get hold of the wonder and reality that they stood in the the front of the purple sea with none way to skip, on the identical time because the Egyptian armies were fast coming near. What did Moses do? He started out out via calming the humans down and reminded them of the God that they served. Now Moses commenced out with the aid of calming down, secondly he began to calm the noise spherical him, for within the midst of false impression or chaos, there can be no answer there, the noise will make you to lose concentration, you'll results get distracted and you'll in no manner see the possibility of turning your scenario proper into a a success one. Thereafter Moses switched and also helped the human beings to recall what they take delivery of as actual with in. The Israelite believed they've a God, however at that very 2nd plenty of them did now not accept as actual with in their God, they believed they may perished at the hands of the Egyptian armies and that there was no way they will flow the red sea. Moses set a exquisite instance of resilience, he knew that there has been always a manner, due to the truth his highbrow sturdiness in no manner failed him, his intellectual sturdiness modified into related to his consider within the God of Israel and that changed into a powerful way of breaking free and escaping from the hands of the Israelites, the resilience of Moses added down the power of God to divide the pink sea and the Israelite went during the ocean to the opportunity end.

If Moses did now not fall lower again on what he believed, there was no manner he may additionally want to are becoming any cease result.

Moses became exceptional the severa Israelite because of the reality he turned into jogging in a high-quality diploma of mentality which one in every of a kind Israelite did not have, Moses have become prepared for the exodus journey, he had such a lot of encounters in his life, from the time he have become a infant. So, the whole thing which you need to turn out to be mentally resilient has to do at the side of your development.

The Israelite once again confirmed their mental weak point once they cried out to Moses that the Egyptian navy were correctly coming after them while the Israelite located out that that that they had crossed to the other facet of the purple sea.

Still they did now not accept as proper with that they are able to in no way be captured through the Egyptians. Sometime those scenario will seem to you in existence, those are moments that touches your diploma of highbrow sturdiness, no longer like Moses, the Israelites saved on complaining, continually lacking the accept as proper with, continually displaying their highbrow weak point, usually displaying naivety, but all of the miracles finished through Moses, they nonetheless had been overwhelmed via fear of being captured.

It took the mental sturdiness of Moses and his trust within the God that he served to hold lower returned the divided Nile to close in at the Egyptian and that modified into their doom.

Listen, it isn't always what's occurring to you that subjects, the actual deal is you, you are the exceptional being stricken by what is going on round you, the way you respond to that scenario is what's going to make human beings evaluate your highbrow durability, that is the easy reality, you can not say you're resilient and also you don't recall inside the possibility of getting some element completed, you may't claim to be mentally difficult or being resilient and also you bitch approximately everything that comes your manner that looks to be causing you misfortune, the time to begin questioning that you may surely triumph over any hassle is now.

Hence, you need to fight lower once more, you want to fight the misfortune without relenting, like the Egyptians who chased Moses, Moses fought again by way of manner of what he knew and trust in, the Pharaoh trusted his military, but Moses trusted his God, he depended on Him collectively with his bear in mind and

Mental toughness, Moses become resilient to the latest chase of the Egyptians and he defeated them.

To be resilient therefore, you want to have a look at the smooth essential things a first-rate way to move an extended way to beneficial beneficial aid your intellectual durability:

•Learn to combat once more

•Don't live down

•Develop a diehard spirit

•Believe in what you've got

•Unleash what you have were given

•Do not be deterred thru your enthusiasts or people around you who don't accept as true with in what you accept as actual with

•Call out that powers inner you

How Determination to Succeed reasons you to become resilient

A man who doesn't have any ambition or plan on how he can attain life has a highbrow weakness. He needs to apprehend his capability and intention better and he can most effective do that at the equal time as he has a better stepped forward mental sturdiness.

How determination does purpose you to come to be resilient? There is one thing this is not unusual to a fulfillment humans who've intellectual durability and that issue is "determination".

Determination is like an contamination inside the thoughts of a individual who desires to come to be mentally hard, on the equal time as you are determined to the volume that you constantly see yourself already living the existence which you want to stay, even as you notice yourself receiving the trophy or gold medal of success, at the equal time as you need to turn out to be a health practitioner, prison expert, entrepreneur, a fulfillment commercial enterprise employer man or woman, or a champion in sports, you do matters a good manner to often float you close and ultimately turning into what you need to be, then you definitely definitely really are decided, you deserve it.

It beats my creativeness as quickly as I see individuals who stay the lifestyles of pauper, I see masses of dad and mom which is probably awful and what baffles me the most is the fact that they may be no longer high-quality and they really don't care to apprehend why they are residing a completely pitiable life. People who absolutely acquire their fate and stay in which they're for decades without any symptoms of improvement are really no longer determined to change their scenario.

If you surely choice to make a change, change will commonly come your way, and that could handiest show up if you are decided to gain the intention, there aren't any strategies about willpower. Believe me if there may be each different manner aside from strength of will, some of human beings will look at that route. Sometimes I'm amused while people communicate approximately appropriate fortune, sure! It's proper you can had been lucky, but you cannot be lucky all the time, that's why you could pay attention from a well-known announcing which is going as consequently "don't constantly count on your fulfillment".

Those who're decided to get a few problem have a few element inner which drives them to fulfillment; it has to do with what they do not forget in and the way they'll be truely worried to get it. Determination will make you to get a few factor which you need via manner of all fee; willpower is a using pressure a good way to propel you to enhance closer to your purpose. If you pay attention to the interviews of a few well-known human beings round the arena, barely will you examine honestly each person who have been given a few element via danger, am not announcing there are not any those who fall into that elegance, no! What I propose is that a few terrific people really acquire what they dreamed of thru being determined to get that trouble which they cherish most.

So in case you are living in in recent times's international and you aren't determined to achieve success, then you definately need to start thinking in a few other manner, you want to boom or start nursing your power of will to be successful.

Determination is one of the characteristics of being resilient and that is the bedrock of development towards accomplishing your purpose.

To be capable of be a decided individual, you want to do the following topics;

•Be resolute to gather your cause

•Write out what you are determined to get

•Start your day through the use of committing to doing matters that will help you accumulate your goals

•Think about your diploma of self-discipline and study yourself

•Each day write out what you've got got been capable of gain even as you were decided

• Create time for silent meditation

• Visualize your self to have already attain your dream desires

• Work inside the course of attaining your intention

• Be ordinary

• Be energetic

Get the favored Motivation

To be resilient you may need motivation, to successfully acquire that intellectual longevity with the aid of the use of way of becoming resilient, you need to preserve up the level, while you decline for your degree of motivation; it will likely be very hard to benefit your purpose desires. Every individual inside the international these days want to have the proper deliver of motivation which should continuously be the first-rate one. That super motivation will make you growth the stress towards becoming resilient and collect mental durability.

Motivation may be performed with the aid of some activities including preference, taking note of motivational audio device, having a mentor and lots of others. In case you growth your desire of undertaking a few detail wonderful, you'll need a shape of motivation, motivation can bring out the very fantastic in you, when you have someone who publications you thru, we have quite pretty a few motivational audio system like Warren Buffet, Robert Kiyosaki, Donald Trump, Bill Gates and so on.

These human beings are a success those who usually deliver out motivational speech and trainings that will help you get the very pleasant level of resilience and intellectual durability to reach any vicinity of your preferred profession.

They are not hard to get right of entry to, they've masses of their speech and trainings on YouTube and you may discover them on social media, they normally supply out their speeches on those systems and you could listen to them or buy their books and take a look at to get stimulated.

Motivation is the spice you need for your lifestyles even as everything seems now not to be jogging, even as you are stimulated, you may go to any duration to carrying out achievement, however fulfillment will no longer come if you aren't inspired to gain fulfillment to your life, so constantly get precipitated in some trouble which you are doing, if you can not have a look at, you could in fact down load motivational movies from video net web sites and you'll get numerous famous individuals who are into motivational speech delivering excellent services on diverse video internet web sites and networks.

Motivation gives you the extra push to simply accept as true with to your ability to attain achievement, being resilient is what makes you tough and people who're very hard will live on in all weather. The problem of many humans is they lack the wanted motivation to transport beforehand of their pairs, reading is a few thing that we collect from the schools and schools, however motivation is a few element that has to do with helping you to be successful and get the critical surrender result, maximum human beings require a few form of push, some get it with out problem a few actually don't get it with out issues, you want to prompt them on, you need to inspire them and this is exactly what takes area round the world, in these days's worldwide we've got champions and we also have individuals who are not champions but mere performers, as an instance, when you have a study many football leagues from one in every of a type international places, you can phrase the difference in some groups more than others, there are organizations who have excessive ability of winning video video video games and that they typically display of their video video games that they may win and they play better than others.

When businesses get inspired they're able to perform at their excellent. Some might also additionally get recommended with economic ensures or rewards and it truly works out for them and that usually gives them the greater push to advantage success.

I'll recommendation that you don't rely upon monetary rewards that allows you to get stimulated. Because motivation must be gotten from a natural source, that is thru the spoken terms, that lengthy vintage approach is what has installed to be very effective, concentrate and listen the phrases of motivation and that allows you to be the important tonic which you need.

When you're being attentive to motivational audio device, ensure you write down the elements which you really want to understand.

What you want to do:

•Create time to be aware about motivational audio system

•Get a pen and a notepad to install writing important records

•Attend seminars and workshops

•Don't recognition on the coins, interest on the motivation and the cash will come

•Get your self acquainted with a motivational speaker

Having a very Strong Ambition

Ambition is the act of meaning to accumulate a few detail that you cherish or hold in excessive esteemed, it's far the preference of an character to gather that beautiful popularity or element that turns into high-quality. Many people around the vicinity live and die with out captivating their goals. It won't be their fault however definitely due to the reality there was no strong ambition.

If you trust that you could accumulate some thing in existence, then you may paintings your ambition to the volume wherein you may be capable of get some thing which you want.

Ambition is one of the the use of strain to propels resilience, while your ambition is constantly emphatic for your thoughts and also you choice it like it is some thing you want to get in any respect rate, with the proper mind-set, be rest assured you can get there in no remote time. It's notable a count number of time earlier than you apprehend it your dreams can be fulfilled, because of this, in anything you do always have a few diploma of ambition, permit it's far a healthful one, there are ambition that can be too immoderate. For instance, in case you preference a huge function in a company, all you want to do is to paintings within the path of conducting it, absolutely do what others aren't doing, earned the area on gain now not through politicking or maneuvering and disposing of your competitor within the enterprise. Your uprightness and similarly ordinary technique in your mission will earn you the promotions a good way to decorate you to get to that degree. That is a few element this is very important, you have to take that significantly.

If you lack the ambition to get some thing that is suitable, you may in no way get it with out trouble. Lack of ambition will first-class go away you day dreaming approximately some factor without getting it. I've have a look at that the ambition hassle is what isn't available inside the lives of maximum human beings.

Michael Jordan come to be once informed throughout his early years as an novice basketball participant that he lacks what it takes to play basket ball, this announcement baffled Michael Jordan, he become informed he cannot play, he took the facts and processed it in his thoughts.

While he have end up sitting feeling rejected, he idea in his thoughts, what is it that is so specific approximately those men that have been selected to play and him neglected and now not determined immediately to play.

Michael Jordan went domestic, he have turn out to be extra formidable and vowed to evidence the team handlers wrong, his ambition spur him to do greater training, and he advanced his abilities, he moved on notwithstanding his preceding disappointments, he worked hard and had been given returned to reckoning, in recent times inside the United states of America and everywhere inside the global, you can not factor out Basketball without speaking approximately the choice Michael Jordan, Jordan have become a circle of relatives name, he proved his reviews wrong, he rose from a no frame to end up any man or woman, his coaches who told him few years decrease lower back that he isn't always suit to play basketball watch and observed him become very well-known and being most of the very quality ever visible within the sports activities activities and additionally pinnacle earner.

Michael Jordan confirmed resilience at the same time as he refused to accept his critique's opinion, and that is going forth to expose that different human beings's opinion doesn't count number quantity in relation to your talents, your highbrow power doesn't rely upon their personal opinion, you're distinct and you could write your private history. Michael Jordan wrote his private facts and he had no opportunity than to move away an indelible mark inside the basketball facts. Whatever you're these days can be transformed into some factor wonderful, you are handiest a raw gold, till you discover yourself, you may certainly shine and discover an area most of the stars.

Become resilient via manner of becoming bold about what you need to acquire or end up. I will offer you with any other instance within the individual of one skilful soccer participant called Ronaldinho, considered one of brazil's famous playmaker and draw near tricksters in the global of football.

Ronaldinho in his early days in soccer pleaded along with his train at the identical time as he emerge as on trial in Portugal to play him. The educate refused and blatantly cautioned Ronaldinho that he doesn't have the peak to play football. Sad, dissatisfied and feeling dejected, Ronaldinho went immediately to increase his abilties, he later have end up the arena's tremendous participant on two events and he have end up said for his trademark capabilities.

Since Ronaldinho isn't gambling worldwide football, his skillful dexterity has been extensively neglected because it appears no person come to be able to re-enact his captivating talents.

Ronaldinho have become ambitious to apply what he has to get what he preferred, he changed into absolutely an fun participant to observe and he exploited his capability by way of the usage of the usage of being resilient and dedicated to his ambition. And this is why he is a respected player in the worldwide of soccer. What do you trust you studied happened to the train who refused to signal Ronaldinho, sighting the truth that he didn't have the heights to play football, the stated teach have come to be voted the worst coach in the international, why? Because he lacked the foresight to peer the expertise and potentials of Ronaldinho at the equal time as he became however to be mounted participant.

This is the lesson you need to understand from the above, you notice, even as you are raw, you are just like a gold which has no longer been delicate, what do I mean?

I'm pronouncing that when you have now not gotten any education, if you have not commenced out out having ambition approximately what you really want, you are just like a uncooked gold which has now not been delicate. Until you begin to construct your ambition, then you'll word that your dreams will hold to increase and turn out to be clearer to you. Ambition therefore is a few aspect that propels an person to continuously need some component and the character will work toward it, even as she or he does that, the tendency that the recurrent attributes of having that issue will become an mindset if you want to normally spur you on, the resilient aspect begins offevolved to turn out to be a characteristic corresponding to your thoughts-set and this is one issue that could force you to excel in your profession.

Ambition therefore is what will assist in enhancing your resilience and your intellectual durability turns into an entire lot more splendid collectively along with your Ambitious inclinations.

Having the Vision

When you have got a vision of what you are doing which is basically futuristic, you may circulate a ways in having the mental toughness, why? Because you'll now not be wondering short time period however all you realise now is long term, for example, I'll give you instances of people round the world who've been successful with what they're doing; it all started out with a vision. These great individuals did no longer definitely begin doing something just due to the truth they preferred to do something for you to keep them busy, as a substitute, they observed the power and brilliant capability in what they may be inventing and in phrases of actualization it could serve a greater reason.

A visionary has the capability to inspect the destiny fulfillment of what she or he is doing. The brothers who invented aero plane sat down together to think about what they may be able to do to collect what that they had visible in a imaginative and prescient approximately flying humans from one location to a few different via the air and they made it rise up and nowadays they're regarded as awesome humans, whilst you lack vision, it approach you cannot satisfy life's given opportunities. The visionary will see thru the future of some thing that he or she is doing, whilst you are able to imaginative and prescient your self and be conscious beyond the ordinary then you may be relaxation assured that success will frequently extend in your thoughts, due to the fact you'll dream to attain everything which you imaginative and prescient about.

Bill Gates idea of some element that could create an interface among humans, some aspect that would motive a document transmission which can cut in some unspecified time in the future of 1 the us of the us to 3 specific and from one continent to each other via the net, he determined a software and made it possible to be accessed by way of way of manner of all and sundry from everywhere inside the worldwide through the internet file switch protocol and it worked.

The entire way started out out out via way of conceiving the concept and vision, in recent times, all of the laptop structures inside the global or all and sundry or enterprise enterprise is using Microsoft office software program program to carry out numerous statistics processing this is beneficial to people and corporation

corporation agency or various establishments. There is not any doubt that Bill Gates and the likes of various people had a vision to make contributions their records to the developing populace of the sector thru genuinely discovering a document transmitting and processing channel so one can be to be had from anywhere inside the global.

Today Bill may be appeared as one of the maximum maximum powerful human beings with the right highbrow sturdiness that we've got had been given within the global these days considering his heritage, while his undertaking and concept became rejected with the aid of approach of various set up corporations, on the same time as he sought to promote his concept to them, he wasn't approximately their rejection of his perception, he in reality went at once to make bigger his skills and discoveries and he earned his success with the aid of believing within the vision that he had surely shared with others who never cared to buy into his idea.

Before your imaginative and prescient can provide you with the results you need, you must consider in the imaginative and prescient, understand that you are the best to look into the future of your proposed concept. It starts offevolved offevolved from you, it doesn't rely whether or now not others buy into it or not, alternatively you'll be the only to shoulder an lousy lot duty of your accept as true with and the vision that includes distinctive sports will truly spur you to overcome what there must be defeated for your manner to achievement. Ask yourself the following query:

•Do I in reality have a vision?

•What is my imaginative and prescient?

•Can I maintain my vision?

•What will I do to keep my vision?

•Do you spot the vision of yourself within the next three hundred and sixty five days, years, 3, years, 5 years and above?

•Will I be capable of get my imaginative and prescient within the path of to others

•Will others apprehend what I dream about

•Can I effect into specific human beings's existence with my vision

•When am I going to apprehend my imaginative and prescient

•When and wherein will I accumulate my imaginative and prescient

Chapter 4: What is intellectual resistance

One of the largest reasons we live a lifestyles of disconnect is because of the

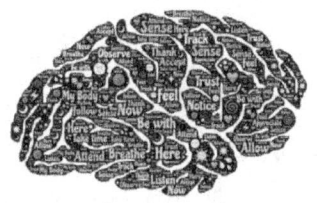

reality we supply round some of emotional and spiritual ache. We also can additionally or won't have a m otive why we do that however, don't forget me; a number of us are in a few kind of ache. Sometimes our hearts are prone and our spirits are damaged, however, though, we upward thrust up and pass about the day and push down the pain. Maybe we were born with religious ache or we've unresolved troubles that we haven't allow flow of and we keep them interior no longer expertise a way to allow bypass. Some be given as actual with in past lives and that we're born with ache and this ache is punishment from a beyond lifestyles. For folks who are Christian, they don't consider this, but believe that we will take away the pain by using giving it to God. Give it to some thing or a person and permit it move when you have it. It's no longer properly well worth protecting immediately to. Without being aware, we maintain on to pain so tight that it leaves us exhausted.

Most of the pain is only in our minds and it's miles a speak we have were given with ourselves. I am no longer pronouncing subjects didn't show up to you to your past. Maybe you may't even bear in thoughts or pin component a few thing. I couldn't bear in mind some of the instances people have long beyond thru and are though capable of stay every day. I even have had hardships, however I am blessed that my pain is not as deep as precise's pain. All pain desires to be allow flow of, even though. The issue proper right here is to offer your self the winning of looking for help to rid your self in case you are in ache. Start sparkling once more, in spite of the fact that for best once on your life. Make the choice to be loose.

Chapter 5: Limiting mind and intellectual programming

Just like every day existence, corporation

or sports activities lifestyles is complicated. Complexity and turbulence are a part of business enterprise and sports sports existence. Relying most effective on information, talents, capacity or beyond success isn't always sufficient. Just like well-known athletes and successful organization leaders, you want intellectual toughness to collect fulfillment.

These talents include:

A hyper attention

This is the functionality to carry out at top levels without giving in to distractions and not the usage of a problem and with readability of mind. This is normally called 'being inside the quarter.'

A Winning Mindset

A prevailing mind-set is an mind-set thru a performer that he ought to win or at least carry out on the most feasible performance diploma, preserving consistency. For a person to try this, he need to have a sturdy notion and religion in his situation information, and abilties no matter the challenges provided to him.

Willpower

As stated earlier, energy of thoughts combines attempt, intention, and braveness. Intention is the 'will' in self-control. It is the insistence on staying at the identical challenge until all the artwork is completed. The attempt you located into doing a little aspect is the energy. It propels you into carrying out what is required of you however the worrying conditions you encounter. Courage is the readiness to undergo up all the worry and one-of-a-kind emotions that you want to carry out the task.

Composed

A mentally hard individual has to hold calm below strain. As the state of affairs heightens and all people else is freaking out, the character remains calm, takes time to assess the scenario after which makes the remarkable possible go with the flow. He ought to stay engaged to the case no matter how excessive the pressure rises.

Lose Nice

Along with the mindset of a winner is the potential to in truth get hold of that the performer is able to failure. Sometimes, notwithstanding the great attention and a wealthy investment of capabilities and assets, a performer can fail to fulfill the set goal. However, the trick lies inside the capability to extract education and values from revel in and to channel it to the subsequent trial, for persisted success.

Own Up

To increase intellectual sturdiness, you want to private as plenty as each state of affairs, each the tremendous and the lousy. A mentally sturdy person is ready and willing to absorb that obligation and stress. He or she believes that no matter the demanding situations and the chances, he or she should provide you with an answer. In case of failure, the character will take inventory, examine his steps to see wherein he went incorrect, collect commands from it, and then bypass on beyond it. This character is aware of how to triumph over terrible emotions and thoughts efficiently.

Preparation

Preparedness entails hundreds of making plans. A performer plans in advance to prepare for any unplanned occasion, throughout, and on the surrender of the event. He or she then creates a backup plan that may be pulled out if definitely the number one plan evaluations massive demanding situations, or that it in fact will now not art work. Planning and steerage of this nature permit the performer to live comfy irrespective of the scenario. In addition, the assignment itself may be in reality recovered and completed while not having to transport lower again to the starting point. What's extra, the groups or the performer's spirit isn't always crashed, and the general universal overall performance rhythm isn't always affected plenty with the aid of manner of the perceived loss and failure.

Ready to Take On the Challenge

A mentally hard individual does not whimper. He does not whine. Whatever comes his way, he without trouble welcomes it. Does it want to live up beyond due to paintings on some assignment work, be it having to tackle more human beings for schooling, be it jogging numerous greater miles? Whatever it's miles, this man or woman has a 'bring it on' mindset, and this produces exposure, revel in, and success.

Stress Optimization

This is the capability to govern strain and stress in an occasion, with none tension, worry or doubt, or at least preserving usual usual performance undeterred with the aid of them. An person who has determined out the manner to optimize pressure will take advantage of a traumatic surroundings and give you outcomes that others could not have provided underneath comparable situations.

Stretch Out the Limits

This is the potential to particular maximum bodily attempt even inside the face of intellectual and bodily pressure. A man or woman can be in pain or physical discomfort and devote himself to provide the first-class popular overall performance however it. We have visible athletes in immoderate bodily pain bypass on to finish the race at the tracks.

A man on the sort of races as soon as tore his knee as he ran the remaining lap. He may have emerged maximum of the pinnacle runners, however his painful knee threw him up to now lower once more. Instead of giving up, and at the same time as even though in excruciating pain, the character began out out limping his way to the give up line. His father, sitting on the pew on the stadium ran up to him and ignoring the protection officials, ran over to his son and supported him. The entire stadium cheered them on until the athlete were given to the completing line.

The athlete blew all and sundry's thoughts with the aid of using way of his intellectual durability and the solve to complete what he had completed. Undoubtedly, he changed into praised and identified better than those who received the race. This is what resilience and sturdiness does; it units you apart from others, even people who can be greater gifted than you're.

Chapter 6: Mental traits of a achievement humans

Successful peoples are first rate at fending off temptation and delaying gratification. They get scared much like everyday people, however they comprehend how to conquer worry in an effort to attain achievement. Unlike ordinary human beings, a achievement human beings don't just prioritize and expect, they start with the maximum important challenge and hold with it until the cease. These characteristics require intellectual sturdiness and energy- and all of the a fulfillment people personal them.

Know and increase the behavior of a fulfillment human beings with intellectual durability:

Always act like you're in average control

A quote from Lgnatius "Hope and pray as although God will cope with all and act as though everything is predicated upon on you." The equal principle applies to success. Many dad and mom assume fulfillment has masses to do with success or failure in existence. If we achieve success, actual fortune desired us and if we fail, achievement changed into in the direction people. The distinction among everyday humans and successful humans that they sense pinnacle fantastic fortune plays some aspect of their achievement, but they don't wait for proper accurate fortune or consider awful correct fortune. They act as even though success or failure simply is predicated upon on them. If they be successful, it's due to the fact they worked hard and inside the occasion that they fail, the tough artwork wasn't enough. One detail they don't do is dropping time questioning what lousy topics may additionally moreover manifest to them. Learn from them and placed all your strive into making things take region, no longer traumatic what ought to arise.

Don't fear approximately subjects you could't exchange

As I truely have stated earlier than intellectual power is like muscle strength and no individual has a huge supply. Don't waste your power and power on topics you can't manage. For some humans, it's the conduct of numerous humans. For others, it's far politics. Whether it's miles your private or expert life, end any challenge with the excellent of your functionality and save you traumatic. You have finished your mission and it's time with a view to loosen up. Things are out of your hand now and traumatic isn't going to change it. This worrying creates needless strain for your intellectual and bodily health and stops the pride and entertainment of life. Studies have established that 80 5% of the time the subjects we fear in no way takes location and if it does take vicinity, eighty% parents cope with the situation better than we belief. Mentally tough human beings can permit flow into unnecessary issues in place of stressing over them.

See the beyond quality as a treasured education session

A quote from unknown scholar "learns from the past, bypass on and grows stronger. People are deceptive however permit your take into account final longer. Do what you want to do, however constantly live right, and in no way permit everyone get the extraordinary of you." Past is treasured, analyze out of your past mistakes and errors of others and bypass on. Letting skip and shifting on is less difficult said than completed and is predicated upon on how you have a have a look at it. When you made a mistake or some detail lousy happens to you, see it as an possibility to study from it. When others make a mistake, you get a hazard to study and function an possibility to be kind and understanding. See the past as education, don't allow it define you. Focus at the winning- at the same time as you targeted at the right right here and now, you will have plenty less time to consider the beyond. Even with all your efforts, beyond disasters certain to creep into your attention time to time, momentarily well known them and produce yourself all over again into the winning scenario. Think about what went incorrect only to analyze and make sure next time you will be higher prepared. If you crowd your mind and live with only hurtful emotions, there may be no room for super thoughts and feelings.

Celebrate the achievement of others

Many folks see fulfillment as a zero-sum recreation. There is best so much to move round, on the same time as someone else is a fulfillment, it in truth technique possible failure for others. This sort of thoughts-set sucks up intellectual strength- energy have to have used to construct a few aspect modern. How we view certainly one of a kind humans's success, is an indicator of our adulthood and notion in our very non-public capacity. When you notice a person is thriving with recognition and opportunities, clients and wins, you discover ways to have a terrific time his or her success. This manner you may find a remedy for the envy, it in reality is one of the reasons of your non-public failure. You get more advantages which incorporates freedom from frustration and fear and greater opportunities to be satisfied.

Don't criticize, whine or complain

Your terms are powerful and function an effect particularly over you. Always whining and criticizing others on your issues makes you experience worse, now not higher. So, if something to your existence is inaccurate, do no longer waste time complaining or criticizing, make use of your highbrow electricity surely and make the scenario higher. Don't waste time whining and thinking. Don't communicate about what's wrong together collectively along with your existence, communicate and take actions to make matters better. Follow the equal method together collectively with your friends and co-employees. Don't restrict your self with the useful resource of being a shoulder they might cry on, proper friends help others to make their existence better.

Count your benefits

Gratitude makes us happier and efficient. Studies have set up that thankful human beings display higher stages of optimism and excessive exceptional feelings, lifestyles delight, and electricity. They enjoy decrease ranges of pressure and despair and much more likely to reap vital personal desires. Every night in advance than you doze off, mirror for your day and grow to be privy to five property you're grateful for. Studies have established education this approach enhance determination, alertness, attentiveness, enthusiasm and electricity.

Chapter 7: Mental conduct and luxury sector

You are all too familiar with the word 'addiction'. You use it to your ordinary communication, and also you apprehend what it manner. You can call them a behavior pattern, a ordinary, or some thing which you do time and again, both consciously or unconsciously. Your day will now not be whole without your dependancy because it's far part of your everyday habitual.

How do conduct artwork? Habits are located out behavior, meaning you are not born with them, you got them from someplace. The whole manner starts offevolved offevolved offevolved with a cue or a trigger. This can be inside the form of time, vicinity, perception, emotion, humans, belief, or conduct. After the motive comes the craving, this is the motivation or choice for the motion. This is then followed with the aid of the motion itself or your response to the craving. After appearing the movement, you get the reward that you are looking beforehand to, and this reward is what drives you to carry out he motion over and over.

Let's illustrate the way of dependancy so that you will understand it better. Let's for instance your addiction is to drink coffee when you awaken. Your motive is waking up within the morning. You drink coffee due to the reality you want to experience massive conscious and alert, this is your yearning. Then your reaction is to drink espresso. Your praise is you feel alert after consuming coffee. Another example is biting your nails, that is a shape of horrible dependancy. The cause is pressure at artwork. Craving is your want to feel calm and on pinnacle of things. Your response is to chunk your nails. Your reward is that you're feeling calmer and more on top of factors while biting your nails.

The Spartans and the Special Operations Units have incredible behavior that make contributions to their amazing basic universal performance. Their behavior are so ingrained of their system that they do the ones behaviors even if they are now not within the army. Take the retired infantrymen, as an example. Waking up in truth early within the morning, getting a crew reduce in choice to a fashionable hairdo, ingesting speedy and with out wastage, and dwelling in simplicity and austerity are behavior that they bring with them even after retirement.

There are styles of conduct—precise conduct and lousy conduct. Of path, you need to keep doing all of your genuine behavior and possibly examine a few new ones. And you need to break your lousy conduct and update them with correct ones.

Forming correct conduct

1.   Start small

To prevent your self from feeling overwhelmed with what you need to advantage, you want to start small. For example, in case you're essential aim is to have a more healthy lifestyle, going from 0 five times in step with week of gym sports or switching to a vegan healthy eating plan from a food regimen loaded with carbs and meat can be too hard to carry out. This can motive a problem in a while because of the truth you may not stay with doing all of your suitable dependancy for a long time due to the reality you feel like you're sacrificing masses. This is why it is important to begin small.

Maybe attempt to visit the gymnasium throughout weekends and cut back to your carbs and chocolates first. When you get used to this, try to tweak it a bit bit and make it extra tough thru going to the fitness center four instances every week and lowering your meat consumption. By slowly easing your self into the dependancy, it will experience natural and normal, as although it has been a part of your normal for a long term.

2.   Make your intentions clean

You want to be clear and unique about what you need to gather if you are clearly critical approximately forming a trendy dependancy. If you endorse out the information of your addiction, you'll maximum probably examine thru to the prevent.

The first element that you may do is to create a time table or cut-off date for your addiction. If it's far important for you, you may truly make time for it. If your agenda is packed in some unspecified time in the future of the day and also you actually can not alternate whatever, why now not awaken a piece in advance so that you have time to do your new addiction, especially if it's miles some element critical.

Another method that you could attempt to make your intentions clean is dependancy stacking. This is linking your new dependancy to an contemporary addiction that is already a part of your normal. You can say "Before going to mattress, I will have a look at a e-book for at least half-hour". By linking the cutting-edge addiction to an antique dependancy, it's miles less tough an awesome way to take into account doing it and it becomes like a continuation of your antique dependancy.

You can also try the implementation intention, in that you hold in mind your dependancy a conditional movement. You can say a few issue like "If I wake up at 6AM, then I will do ten pushups."

3.   Get hooked

Have you ever been so engrossed in a book that you cease it in best one night time time? Have you commenced a undertaking which you in reality like doing and also you locate it hard to prevent operating on it? This is the identical with conduct. You form behavior due to the reality you get hooked on doing them. So, make certain which you find out a way to get addicted to doing all your addiction.

One approach that you can attempt is the "don't break the chain" method. Whenever you end doing the dependancy for the day, you can mark a huge X to your calendar. You can also use stickers to track your dependancy. This will encourage you to do your addiction every day, with out missing an afternoon due to the truth you do no longer want to break the chain and you do not need to appearance in the end in your calendar without the large X. Having a visible reminder is a brilliant way to shape a superb dependancy. And because the chain grows longer, it will be extra difficult to interrupt it due to the reality you recognize that you have already invested quite some attempt in it and breaking it's miles a large waste of time and effort for your element.

4.   Change your environment

Your surroundings has a big part in growing behavior. Consider the Spartans and the Special Operations Units. Their environments are not always snug, however they may be effective in forming appropriate conduct and breaking bad ones. For instance, the beds they sleep in aren't exactly lodge cloth. But it honestly works because it allows them to awaken early each morning and to normally be alert, a few element that they have to do even though they may be napping.

You moreover need to discover approximately the activation energy, or the quantity of power required getting some thing completed. The extra activation electricity is wanted, the less in all likelihood you'll do the movement and stick to it. And vice versa. For example, if you need to check extra books, make certain books are available in each room of your house. If you located away your books in a glass-enclosed shelf with lock and key, then forming the addiction of analyzing can be greater tough. Make it less difficult with a view to do your habit.

five.   Be accountable

If you are held liable for your actions, you are maximum probable to paste to doing all your behavior. One real idea is to make your purpose public. Tell your own family or friends about what you are attempting to achieve, whether or not it's miles ingesting extra healthy, getting greater exercising, and minimizing impulse shopping for, waking up early, and so forth. By letting human beings apprehend approximately your plans, you'll enjoy greater obligated to have a look at thru because of the truth you do now not want to embarrass yourself and allow people count on that you are all talk and no substance. You can also find out an obligation companion who will assist you music your development and make you stay along with your plan.

Remember how the Spartan women deal with guys at the equal time as training? They teased and ridiculed guys to steer them to perform properly. You do now not necessarily want someone to shame you in reality to make you do what you need to do due to the fact this is an immoderate method however at the least try to find out a pal who will no longer allow you to pass off path each time you enjoy like slacking off.

Soldiers additionally have buddies whilst training who help them get through the unique duties but additionally boosts their morale once they experience down. And you ought to of route do the equal detail in your obligation partner if he is also in the manner of developing a modern day addiction.

6. Make it part of your self

Habits are a part of a person's identity. You associate the addiction to the person and occasionally it's miles what the man or woman is idea for. When someone asks you about your buddies, you'll say a few issue like, "I genuinely have a chum who likes to exercise and goes to the health club ordinary" or "There's this pal of mine who can't feature the least bit without ingesting her cup of coffee first". Or even as you're asked to tell greater statistics about yourself, you may likely say a few issue like "I make it a thing to finish my vital responsibilities first in advance than I waft immediately to the less complex ones". These are all behavior and also you select out human beings, which consist of yourself, with them.

If you begin thinking of an movement as part of your self, it's far going to be less hard so that it will maintain on with it without the need for everyday reinforcement. Make it part of yourself that makes you a unique person.

Breaking terrible conduct

Habits are part of your ordinary lifestyles, this is why they may be tough to interrupt. Bad behavior have constantly been a topic of mental research and studies because of the reality they have got horrible influences on a person's life. It maintains them from accomplishing their goals and it additionally interrupts with their life. Bad conduct also aren't actual to your health and they will be only a waste of belongings together with time, strength, and coins.

Two of the foremost causes of bad conduct are boredom and strain. Sometimes, people do not have some thing better to try this they begin doing some thing that later on will become a lousy dependancy. For instance, you buy groceries someday because of the truth you experience bored and you discovered out it felt nicely to shop for stuff and it turns into a addiction whenever you sense bored. Or occasionally, you revel in harassed which you want to do some thing advantageous approximately it, which include biting your nails. You need to understand the motive of your horrible dependancy and get to the inspiration of the hassle so that you can higher address it.

So how do you smash a terrible habit? Here are a few mind.

1.   Replace it with an extremely good addiction

Sounds clean, however it is genuinely greater hard than you consider you studied. Sometimes, opposing conduct, one suitable and the opportunity horrible, have the same prevent-result. For example, you smoke each time you feel confused out. It calms your nerves. But of direction, smoking isn't always exceptional for your fitness. So, try and find out an possibility.   Maybe   try   breathing techniques for alleviating stress. Or attempt meditation. Another awful addiction is establishing Facebook whilst you're feeling bored. Instead of studying vain facts in your newsfeed, why not perform a bit element else a good manner to venture you mentally, like analyzing a ebook or answering a crossword puzzle. You may also even carry out a hint brief physical sports. There are such a whole lot of options that you can take into account. Just recognize what triggers your craving that results in awful behavior, and from there, provide you with special behaviors as a way to satisfy that craving.

2.   Try to cast off triggers

Ask yourself what triggers your conduct? Once making a decision the cause, try and cut it to make the awful dependancy go away. For example, in case you discover yourself carrying out for that bottle of alcohol every time you sense lonely, it way your motive is the feeling of loneliness. You can cast off that feeling of loneliness via engaging in out to your loved ones or getting to know a hobby, which can update your addiction of eating. Keep in mind that dependancy is not the same as dependancy. If you are addicted, because of this you are already an alcoholic, you need to are searching for expert help.

If the sight of clothes on the mall triggers your impulse to shop for, then do not visit the mall. You can't definitely take away the mall from its place, but you can virtually avoid it.

3.   Cold turkey answers may not constantly paintings

Doing a few detail cold turkey is doing it proper away, without easing your self step by step into the behavior. For instance, if you have been smoking for ten years nowadays, identifying to prevent smoking beginning the following day is a cold turkey answer. You will nice discover your self taking a gasp after some days and beginning the terrible addiction once more because of the fact bloodless turkey answers make topics into particular black and white regions. This way that it pleasant perspectives the lousy dependancy as some issue a hundred% terrible, even as in reality, terrible conduct moreover deliver a few element first-rate. Smoking, for instance, makes someone revel in calm and helps relieves pressure, even though it is in truth awful for the health. This is why it's miles critical to take this into interest in desire to right away removing that one detail that makes you experience higher.

Moreover, going cold turkey moreover locations emphasis on perfection. And perfection is some thing this is tough to advantage. One mistake which you make already makes your complete plan a failure. Try to offer yourself a chunk wiggle-room particularly when you have been doing the dependancy for many years.

Going cold turkey isn't constantly a failure in terms of breaking a awful addiction. In fact, some of people have finished it earlier than. Some stopped smoking proper away with out giving an excessive amount of thought approximately it, but they may be able to stick with it. These are robust-willed people, much like the Spartans and the Special Forces. Of route, you may furthermore be like them, if you decorate your strength of mind, which has been stated intensive within the preceding chapters.

You can integrate the techniques cited in forming suitable behavior with the guidelines for breaking lousy behavior. They move hand in hand. And in case you do them together, you may discover it less complicated to acquire your goals.

You can also want to realize the splendid behavior of the Spartans and the Special Forces that motive them to great warriors and soldiers.

Habits of Spartan warriors and elite squaddies which you need to strive

Cold shower in the morning

You already recognise via now that the Spartans took cold showers within the morning. Doing this helped assemble their iron field because it permits your body get used to pain. And even as your body can endure pain, you may not effortlessly offer in to temptations and impulses, accordingly appreciably improving your strength of will. You need to moreover encompass this in your each day addiction in case you want to do it the Spartan manner.

Always have an get away plan or plan B

Special Forces continually survey the place short for escape routes in case of an attack or ambush. Although it is not a not unusual prevalence to be attacked, it's far nonetheless a extremely good addiction to make bigger particularly in recent times whilst the location is lots more risky. Going in your favored Starbucks might be some factor that you do on a daily basis and you sense cushty going to the vicinity, but you need to learn about emergency exits the subsequent time you skip lower returned to buy coffee.

In relation to having an escape plan, you have to actually have a backup plan or plan B or however you need to name it in case your initial plan didn't exercise consultation. For instance, in case you are thinking about taking place a journey overseas, however you're although not positive if you could take off from art work for severa days, you must have an opportunity plan, like taking region a neighborhood tour. Preparing for some element that could rise up aside from your preliminary plan is a few aspect which you must grow to be a addiction to prevent disappointments and frustrations.

Intermittent fasting

For the Spartan warriors, consuming isn't always finished for pride. It is a need used to fuel their frame to complete their education and for after they go to war. The Spartans didn't wake up in the midnight and go to the kitchen for a midnight snack or munch on a few issue when they enjoy bored. And neither do the Special Forces. They consume because they need to no longer because of the reality they need to. Intermittent fasting is a addiction that the Spartans practiced. While on fasting, your senses may be more sensitive to stimuli and you will be on immoderate alert. After eating, you will feel like resting and you aren't in the mood to do some thing. This does now not advocate that you need to no longer eat because of route you want meals to stay but exceptional devour what your frame wishes for nourishment. Moreover, quite a few studies display that intermittent fasting is powerful if you are trying to lose weight. It actually has pretty a few blessings. No surprise the Spartans did its loads of years within the beyond.

You can strive some issue like now not ingesting some thing from 8PM to twelve midday. This is easy due to the truth you sleep most of the time in the path of those hours. You also can strive doing it alternately, at some point you can flow fasting and the subsequent you will consume usually. It is as a great deal as you what you determined will paintings amazing however that is a splendid addiction to pick out out up because it promotes eating most effective what your body desires and it prevents you from eating unnecessarily.

Start your day early

Soldiers are seemed for being early risers. You will already see them up and approximately even earlier than the sun rises. And they're no longer like most folks that are although 1/2 of of asleep after you've got up. They are alert and already being powerful. Most of them spend the number one waking hour of their day on foot because of the reality they want to preserve their blood flowing first difficulty inside the morning. Jogging within the morning isn't always only a remarkable cardio exercise. It furthermore will increase your intellectual alertness all through the day. It permits you get prepared for the day's obligations. Moreover, through the usage of waking up early, you will be in a feature to accomplish extra and additionally end responsibilities early on.

However, now not in reality all people are early risers no matter what they do. They clearly function higher at some stage in middle of the night. There's now not whatever wrong with this, as long as you end what desires to be accomplished on time. It is without a doubt favored through the navy to wake up early because not a few aspect beats getting up early within the morning and taking walks out of doors to the sound of birds chirping and just at the same time as the solar is prepared to upward push.

Heavy lifting 3 instances in keeping with week

If you want to look like a Spartan warrior or a army guy, you ought to begin working on those muscle companies via lifting heavy weights as a minimum three times in keeping with week. Do no longer drift proper now for those small dumbbells, observed with the aid of bicep curls. You should observe an effective software for lifting weight, at the side of StrongLifts 5x5 that specializes in your power and length. You should spend some time doing the deadlift, the bench press, the overhead press, and the squat. Increase the depth of your workout with the resource of along with more weight and counts on your present day-day exercising. This will now not handiest improve your body, strength, and stamina. It might also make you mentally hard because of the fact you're capable of go through a bodily exercise of this depth severa days in in keeping with week.

Good grooming

This isn't about arrogance however extra about being presentable and terrific-looking. If you want human beings to take you notably, you want to appearance the element, in particular if you are trying to scare off enemies. You do now not normally want to buzz lessen but always make certain that your hair is trimmed. For men, lengthy hair handiest receives inside the manner and is also hard to keep so maintain it quick usually. You do now not need to waste some time styling your hair each day. Aside from hair, you want to additionally be privy to what you wear. Have you visible a soldier sporting wrinkled garments? Make sure your garments are ironed in advance than you put on them. Trim your nails regularly due to the truth prolonged nails are a no-no. Always attempt to appearance your exquisite wherever you flow into even at the identical time as you're at domestic because of the truth while you look suited, you may additionally enjoy accurate about

your self it simply is a brilliant raise of self
belief.

Chapter 8: Emotion code

Now that we've mentioned a number of the overriding thoughts which motive more degrees of mental durability, along with coping with worry and stress inside the proper manner, further to developing higher conduct. It's time to have a look at a few practical techniques to collect this to your ordinary existence. The first of it's miles mastering the manner to reason set properly. This concept very a bargain compliments forming better conduct, as it offers a blueprint to direct your everyday sports and behaviors in a greater amazing fashion. To maintain you at the proper music and out of trouble.

So many guru's and instructors get this incorrect in phrases of goal setting in my opinion. They frequently u . S . A . That dreams should be fantastically particular in terms of what someone desires I.E. Certain logo of watch they need, particular corporation feature or specific dollar amount of cash of their financial organization account. But moreover, in exactly what time-body they wish to gain it via I.E. In three months or thru some set in stone date.

Whilst I receive as true with this wondering to 3 diploma, particularly almost approximately shorter term goals. I accept as true with its awful advice for the bigger topics, the longer term desires you need to obtain. Let me inform you why. The human mind in reality does no longer art work on this manner. The unconscious thoughts, it's in the end chargeable for supplying the possibilities to actualize the ones achievements, does now not work in specifics. It works in photographs, emotions and feelings as an alternative.

In this experience, its a protracted way higher to split motive installing location into segments, the near time period vs the long time, as each categorizes require a fantastic mode of questioning to complete (aware forebrain hobby for the previous, and subconscious "under the ground" hobby for the latter). So, allow's begin with the resource of exploring the mechanisms through which we achieve those instant milestones. But in advance than we do, I want to issue out that I find out that there is lots poor connotation in the direction of the phrase "motive" in fashionable. It smells of employer jargon or self-help verbiage, which locations people off from ever jotting them down to start with.

I usually discover the phrase "intention" higher describes quick term dreams, as they're literal targets on a dartboard, which you can zero into with complete clarity. I furthermore find out that "assignment" has a greater legitimate enjoy on the subject of the loner time period dreams, as they encompass a larger body of labor spanning some years in most instances. This word more correctly describes the manner wherein maximum humans function (which includes myself) whilst striving for his or her remaining life motive. But lets start with the fast stuff first.

Short Term Targets (1-3 months)

This is the proper time to be highly precise. These are the tangible KPI style metrics you may come across in a data access interest as an instance. You also can want to collect certain benchmarks each day, week or month. This is relevant despite the fact that, as you require short time period desires to cause at to ensure maximum productivity. But moreover, as a way to gauge quick time period improvement. Similar to the dolphin analogy I referred to previously, you want to be installing those goal parameters before steamrolling for 1-three months and knocking them down as you move.

Have you ever at a loss for words why it's difficult to lose look in advance to no actual reason? However, when you have to healthy into that bridal ceremony get sporting 6 weeks time, then all of a stunning it will become that lots less hard. The cause is that the thoughts has a particular target to intention at, and a hardwired time-body through the use of which to reap it thru. This works for some thing indoors a ninety-day term. I.E. Getting wholesome for an upcoming triathlon, studying for an essential examination and so forth. The thoughts want to conceive the motive in reality and consider it can be completed. Then you could paintings towards it with enough recognition and motivational juice to get you to the quit line.

This is why the ones goals SHOULD be quantifiable and time unique. The conscious and rational wondering centers of the mind can completely interpret those metrics and formulate actual A to B plans to achieve them. They additionally make certain the everyday go together with the go along with the float of small wins which may be so critical on your highbrow state. It induces the regular release of experience right hormones and mood regulators which incorporates serotonin & dopamine. However, this is in which short time period targets lead to their effectiveness.

Long Term Projects (5-10 years)

When you're set on improving your very very own intellectual durability, you need to clearly apprehend how the human mind works. This is specially actual while coping with longer time horizons. Larger and loftier life goals should be grandiose; they must be hyper-formidable. Think of it like aiming for the horizon line, it certainly is tough to gain in truth, because it's a hypothetical element. That's exquisite though, as those reason pushed desires are so huge and ambitious, they aren't imagined to be hit. If you shoot for the celebs, you'll probable hit the moon. But that's better then aiming for the moon and by no means leaving earths orbit. These aspirations will consists of things like "turning into extraordinarily wealthy" or "becoming a global elegance organisation chief" or "having a large and incredible family".

It's very tough to quantify these gadgets definitely. Exactly how an lousy lot cash constitutes being "quite wealthy"? What function do you preserve in what enterprise? Exactly what number of children, grandchildren are you going to have? The thoughts works with images and emotions concerning those instances. A a protracted way higher method for long time desires is to create a image or film on your thoughts approximately what these things may need to appear to be. How do you appearance and feel as quickly as you have done this stuff? What are you carrying? What automobile are you the use of? How does your posture now look?

The mind can not differentiate amongst beyond, present and destiny activities on the situation of images in the mind. If you related sufficient emotional context and feeling to what you are playing on your minds eye I.E. A past memory or projected destiny occasion, the body elicits precisely the equal biochemical reaction, as though that revel in became taking place proper now. It's a clever trick that can persuade the thoughts into believing which you have already accomplished those objects. The unconscious will then visit artwork in serving up greater and comparable opportunities to deliver into your bodily reality.

The Fortune Teller vs The Forecaster

Another reason you ought to no longer be setting precise figures and time-frames on those massive dreams, is again because of obstacles of the human thoughts. The aware mind and rational cortexes feature wonderfully as trouble solving mechanisms however is largely set-as much as assume in linear terms. Progress is taken into consideration as a consistent nation increase, in phrases of a difficult and speedy percent I.E. 30% consistent with 365 days. However, in truth, matters do no longer play out like this in the real international with respect to development and success.

In this enjoy, people are horrible long term forecasters. We are essentially akin to fortune tellers while we try to do this. Warren Buffet is famous for putting forward that "Forecasts may also moreover assist you to recognize a super deal about the forecaster, but they allow you to comprehend no longer a few component approximately the future". This is because of the reality we generally overestimate what we are able to accumulate in 1-2 years. But notably underestimate what may be finished in ten years. We presume the linear progress will hold in a straight line.

But in fact, this improvement starts offevolved underneath our initial expectations for the primary 2-three years. Projects of a wide variety take extra time and effort to get off the floor than we first of all anticipated. But if we persist through this point, the magic begins offevolved to arise. At throughout the five yr mark, the rubber truely begins offevolved to hit the road. Momentum starts offevolved offevolved to collect exponentially as possibilities upward thrust up at ever growing fees. This compounding effect approach we commonly become way higher on the development chart in comparison with our initial linear predictions. We have frequently miscalculated via a difficulty of 50-one hundred instances!

This is once more why we must not be forecasting specifics almost about large tasks. We are nearly honestly undercutting ourselves if we do. All of this stuff are way off your radar indicates to begin with. No one is sensible sufficient to because it want to be expect in which they'll be in a decade's time, specifically in current-day worldwide in which trade is going on faster than at whenever in human facts. It's like trying to forecast the climate. You ought to make reasonably correct predictions for the following couple of hours I.E. Shorter time period targets. But some thing beyond this point turns into an knowledgeable guess at tremendous.

You also can even find that you can begin to pivot after a number of years. You might probably see yourself managing a network restaurant, but after numerous years you decide to begin a restaurant of your very own. These subjects commonly come into your life while it's the right time for you. Stating that you need to begin a hairdressing preserve in 3 years from now is probably a horrible time a exquisite manner to actualize this. It might be too early or too late in phrases of your experience. This is once more why you shouldn't positioned time limits on those big desires.

I'm now not offering you with a inexperienced moderate to procrastinate all of the time earlier than beginning that lifestyles purpose task. You can constantly find out excuses for now not doing it, however in your coronary coronary heart of hearts, you'll recognize at the equal time as you're equipped. If you truely focus at the mental photograph of reaching it frequently enough, after which positioned inside the steady and required art work on a every day foundation, it's going to show up in your reality while it's the best time for you. "Fall in love with the manner, and the consequences will deal with themselves" as they're saying.

Again, achieving proper mental energy has little to do with momentary bursts of motivation or braveness. They help in some every day instances to aid in overcoming minor obstacles. But the bigger and further extraordinary achievements are attained through making the diffused, however big adjustments on your thinking over the long time. To improve your behavior and set out dreams to guide you consequently. Then it's approximately installing the continual art work and application as commonly. This is the pleasant way to make certain success, and now not go away some thing to chance.